R.D. Bartlett and Patricia P. Bartlett

Turtles and Tortoises

Everything About Selection, Care,
Nutrition, Housing, and Behavior

With Full-color Photographs
Illustrations by Michele Earle-Bridges

BARRON'S

CONTENTS

UNDERSTANDING YOUR TURTLE OR TORTOISE

Chelonians—a broad term that means both turtles and tortoises— are responsive pets with modest needs. Your local grocery, pet, and hardware stores can supply everything you (and your pets) will need for housing, supplies, and food.

Aquatic Turtles

The aquatic turtles have webbed toes and spend the majority of their time in the water. These include

✔ basking turtles (here, "basking" means the turtles crawl out onto logs or rocks to sun themselves) of the family Emydidae, which are the sliders

✔ spotted turtles
✔ painted turtles
✔ cooters
✔ map turtles.

Most aquatic turtles are species of freshwater habitats, but a few are estuarine or brackish water forms. A few terrestrial species, such as the box and the wood turtles, are also included in this family.

Like all members of the genus, the Escambia map turtle is a powerful and agile swimmer.

Non-basking Aquatic Turtles

The "non-basking" aquatic turtles include
✔ mud and musk turtles (family Kinosternidae)
✔ snapping turtles (family Chelydridae)
✔ soft-shelled turtles (family Trionychidae)
✔ side-necked turtles (families Chelidae and Pelomedusidae).

These turtles often sun themselves by floating at the water's surface or atop a patch of floating weeds, but occasionally do emerge from the water to bask on a sloping bank or an exposed branch.

Landbound Chelonians

The tortoises are exclusively landbound chelonians of the family Testudinidae. Generally, the tortoises have highly domed shells. A few, such as the pancake and hinge-back tortoises, have lower silhouettes. The forefeet of burrow-

This young female leopard tortoise, Geochelone p. pardalis, *is eating shards of eggshells to help with calcium intake.*

ing species may be flattened from back to front and spadelike for digging. Collectively, tortoises are awkward swimmers at best and can easily drown if they accidentally stumble into water that is too deep for escape.

Start-Up Concerns

How much of an investment does it take to get started in turtle- or tortoise-keeping? It depends to a large extent on how much space you want to devote to the setup and how much you'd like to spend. Of course, you want and need caging that provides the best possible space for your pet at the most reasonable investment of time and money on your part. The best news is that getting started isn't prohibitively expensive.

Once you're all set up, how long will your pet live? When properly maintained, it is not unusual for captive turtles or tortoises to live for more than 20 years.

TIP

Recognizing Hunger

A turtle or tortoise that is hungry generally seems to be restless, and moves about its enclosure, nosing at objects it encounters. Unfortunately, a chelonian that has gone without proper food for too long becomes weakened and apathetic; food that is offered too late may not be recognized or eaten, even when placed in full view.

Your Pet's Needs

Like any other living creature, your pet turtle or tortoise needs the three basics—food, water, and shelter. But these three categories mean different things to different types of turtles and tortoises.

Food

Food not only provides energy for immediate needs, but maintains the turtle's health and provides for future growth. As turtles get older, their dietary preferences may change. Learn about your pet. For instance, many sliders begin their lives as omnivores, accepting and seeking out insects, worms, and crunchy bits of underwater vegetation or surface-floating plants like duckweed. This preference is reflected in captivity as well as in the wild. Baby sliders will occasionally snack on tank vegetation or romaine lettuce as well as animal matter. As they mature, they'll become more vegetarian, dining primarily on your aquarium plants, floating leaves of romaine lettuce, or any other dark-green lettuce; do not feed iceberg lettuce, which doesn't offer enough nutrition for your pet. Occasionally you may still want to offer thawed frozen smelt, trout chow, or a pelleted turtle food.

Tortoises are essentially vegetarians throughout their lives, but prefer a wide variety of vegetables and fruit, and the occasional change generally gets a good response. Land turtles, such as box turtles, generally don't change their dietary habits, continuing to feed upon earthworms, apples, romaine, and tomatoes, with an occasional treat of softened kibble dog food.

Water

No matter what kind of chelonian you have, it needs water, if only to drink.

Aquatic turtles will dehydrate, dry up, and die if kept dry and allowed only enough water to drink. They need enough clean water to fully submerge and swim. Many kinds of aquatic turtles cannot swallow food unless they are submerged, no matter how hungry they may be.

Semiaquatic turtles need enough water to occasionally clamber in and become wet all over, although they do not need to be in water to eat. Their enclosures must be slightly more humid than those for the tortoises, and a "bathing-size" water dish will help keep the humidity high enough.

Tortoises and terrestrial turtles need a slightly smaller water dish, but these chelonians must always have clean water available to drink.

Shelter

Although chelonians thermoregulate by sunning, they seek places of seclusion when it comes time to sleep. If no secluded area is provided, tortoises will sleep, nose in, in a corner of their pen. Depending on the weather, our tortoises sleep under low-growing bushes in their enclosure or inside their tortoise house. Turtles often sleep submerged but clinging to vegetation or twigs, so that the surface is not more than a few inches away. Provide an area where they can sleep underwater and yet feel secluded. Semiaquatic turtles, such as wood turtles, will sleep under grass mounds or burrowed into clumps of sphagnum.

Behavior

Unlike many other reptiles such as snakes or iguanas that respond to an implied threat by biting or lashing with the tail, chelonians withdraw into their shells. They are easily fright-

This albino western painted turtle is owned by Clive Longden.

ened; if possible, aquatic types simply may swim away quickly. Once frightened into their shells, new captives are slow to emerge, and any fast movement on your part is apt to make them withdraw again. Chelonians are also sensitive to loud noises, vibrations, and sudden bright lights.

Defenses

If the species involved have somewhat reduced shells (snapping and musk turtles) or otherwise modified shells (soft-shelled turtles and pancake tortoises), they have usually developed an alternate means of defense such as strong jaws and claws or increased agility.

Chelonians of many species have developed other ploys, from camouflage to biting, as additional safeguards.

TIP

A Silent Predator

Although the findings are not yet conclusive, it is likely that the various fire ants are among the most serious predators of turtles and tortoises. This is especially so in the United States, where, since introduced fire ants have no natural enemies, they are now more numerous acre by acre than even in their native tropical American strongholds.

The problem is this: The natural reaction of most turtles and tortoises to pain is to withdraw into their shells and remain stationary until the offending object has left. If this reaction is in response to a fire ant attack, the turtle can soon be overcome and killed by the insects.

But the ants attack more than the adult chelonians. Fire ants are especially effective at locating hatching eggs and overcoming the emerging baby chelonians. The various American box turtles are among the species most seriously threatened by the ever increasing fire ant scourge. Although total eradication of fire ants is now unlikely, stringent control of fire ant populations in wild areas is of paramount importance to both wildlife and humans.

Camouflage

Just try to make out the outline of a big leopard tortoise resting in the dappled shade beneath a shrub or that of an Indian star tortoise in the tangled grasses of a dry savanna. Or try to find the domed, algae-covered carapace of a mud turtle in the water-smoothed,

Unusual in that it has a pattern of radiating markings, this is a pretty red-footed tortoise.

algae covered stones of a pond bottom; the carapace of a snapping turtle in the submerged snags and detritus of its pond-bottom home; or the vague outline of a soft-shelled turtle, buried under sand. Camouflage works!

Shells

The shells of many turtles and tortoises are modified to provide varying degrees of protection. The plastron (bottom shell) of New World mud turtles has two hinges that allow it to be drawn upward. Since, even when thus closed, the small plastron does not entirely cover the soft parts, the value of the hinges seems questionable. In contrast, the large, singlehinged plastron of the American and Asiatic box turtles provides nearly complete protection. African mud turtles also have a fairly large, single-hinged plastron that provides considerable (but not complete) protection when closed.

TIP

Signs of Illness

Chelonians that are ill tend to stay withdrawn in their shells, which makes not only diagnosis but treatment and feeding difficult. For more information on choosing a healthy turtle or tortoise, see the next chapter. For information on treating a turtle or tortoise that is ill, see pages 18–21.

Few tortoises have a hinged plastron. Of these few tortoises, the plastral hinge of the seldom seen little spider tortoise of Madagascar is best developed.

Of all turtles and tortoises, only the members of the African tortoise genus Kinixys, all aptly called hinge-backed tortoises, have a carapacial (top shell) hinge. When drawn against the plastron, the steeply domed posterior carapace helps protect the rear limbs and tail.

When startled or threatened, some turtles and tortoises withdraw their heads into their shells and fold their usually heavily scaled forelimbs across the anterior shell opening. This is especially well noted among the more terrestrial (wood and leaf turtles) species.

Other Defenses

There are some turtles that are simply unable to withdraw their heads. Among these, the skull is often massive and the mandibles formidably strong (big-headed and snapping turtles). In some cases, the neck is also elongated (common

On warm, sunny days, cooters and related turtles bask in abandon, limbs fully extended and feet splayed widely.

snapping turtle), providing a great reach when a defensive bite is attempted.

Additional Defenses

Many of the more secretive aquatic and semiaquatic species have additional defenses. The odor from scent glands gives the musk turtles their common names of "stinking-Jims" or "stinkpots." If lifted or carelessly handled, many turtles, especially the snappers and soft-shells, kick and scratch with long legs and sharp claws.

Some turtles that seem rather poorly adapted for protection through striking and biting indulge in defensive posturing (fully extended hind legs), thus tilting their shell toward the aggressor and lunging forward. This "butting" motion apparently acts as a predator deterrent.

The largely unprotected heads and necks of the sideneck turtles seem curiously vulnerable. Although in many cases the extra length of the carapace and the plastron offers protection from above and below, from the front the neck and head are virtually unprotected. Perhaps camouflage, cryptic coloration and markings, and the exudate from the scent glands deter most predators. The various aquatic soft-shelled turtles of the family Trionychidae also have long necks and formidable jaw power.

Hiding

Baby tortoises and turtles of both aquatic and terrestrial species are more secretive than the adults. Tortoise babies often remain in grassy or brushy cover, box and wood turtles amidst leaf litter and woodland detritus, and aquatic species

Sliders bask on all kinds of projecting materials. From these, they can quickly slide if startled.

near or amid submerged vegetation and thick snags. Babies of sedentary aquatic species (snappers and soft-shells) hide in submerged fallen leaves or bury themselves in the muddy/sandy substrate of their ponds and rivers.

Eyesight

Turtles and tortoises have very acute eyesight and the merest movement of a distant (potential) predator will send basking aquatics into the water or cause strolling terrestrials to become quiescent. No matter what size or age they may be, turtles instinctively know that being overlooked by predators is, quite simply, the best defense of all.

Of the several subspecies, the ornate diamond-backed terrapin, **Malaclemys terrapin macrospilota,** *is usually the prettiest.*

CHOOSING A HEALTHY SPECIMEN

Turtles and tortoises are well known for their habit of withdrawing into their shells for long periods. This habit may make assessing the health of a given specimen difficult—especially for a novice.

What to Look For

More so than captive bred ones, wild specimens are especially prone to withdrawing their head, limbs, and tail from sight. Tortoises are often even more retiring than turtles, further complicating the selection process.

What should you look for when considering the purchase of a turtle or tortoise? How does the appearance of a healthy specimen differ from that of an ill one? And, if the specimen does withdraw, what then?

All things, including the agility with which the animal withdraws its soft parts and the persistence with which it remains hidden must be considered when choosing a turtle or tor-

For a size comparison, a hatchling razor-backed musk turtle, Sternotherus carinatus, sits on the back of an adult male.

toise. There are a couple of things that you should pay attention to even when it is withdrawn, and there is a nonthreatening trick or two that you can use to induce the turtle or tortoise to cooperate.

✔ First, slowly approach the specimen in which you are interested. To a chelonian that is already frightened by capture and caging, the presence of any large approaching shape implies danger. A fast-moving large shape is usually considered more dangerous than a slow-moving or stationary one.

✔ If you move slowly, you may be able to approach rather closely without inducing a complete withdrawal by the specimen.

✔ If the turtle is a type normally associated with water, it is less likely to withdraw fully if it is submerged than if it is out of water.

✔ Once touched, a frightened turtle will remain withdrawn longer than if not touched.

As evidenced by this adult Florida chicken turtle, turtles are able to withstand and recover from a tremendous amount of trauma to both shell and limbs.

Eyes

If you are able to see the turtle's or tortoise's eyes, are they bright and clear? They should be—even if the turtle is beneath the water's surface. If out of water, the turtle's eyes should have neither exudate nor encrustations around or beneath them, nor should the eyelids be puffy and swollen. Does the animal follow your movements with its eyes? It should.

Breathing

There should be no bubbling or wheezing from the nostrils, even when the head is quickly withdrawn. Either of these manifestations probably indicates a respiratory ailment. The turtle/tortoise should be breathing normally (through its nostrils with mouth closed) rather than gasping with an open mouth. Open-mouth breathing indicates nasal passage obstructions. These are most often associated with a respiratory ailment.

Swimming

If in the water, does the turtle submerge easily and fully and retain an even keel when submerged and swimming? Or, does the turtle float like a cork with one side higher than the other? If your answer is yes to the first question and no to the second one, all is probably well. If you have answered no to the first part and/or yes to the second, the specimen in question may have problems. Respiratory distress can result in the specimen's swimming on an uneven keel or bobbing on the surface and failing to submerge. Do not purchase the specimen.

Visible Clues

Aquatic species should be checked to assure there are no open wounds or fungus-covered bruises on its soft parts. Although most external fungi are easily eradicated, there is no reason to start out with a problem. Fungus may appear either as a fuzzy cottony growth or as a rather smooth, velvety sheet. Do not confuse fungal infections (white chlorophyll-free growths) with algal growths. The latter are usually green and grow on the shell (more rarely the limbs) of highly aquatic turtle species. Algal growths are harmless.

Lift the Turtle or Tortoise

Unless it is a soft-shelled turtle or a pancake tortoise, its shell should be firm (hatchlings) to rigid (adults). The shells of soft-shelled turtles (*Apalone* species) and the pancake tortoise (*Malacochersus tornieri*) are naturally softer and more pliable than the shells of other turtle and tortoise species. The shells of the hatchlings of all species are somewhat less firm than those of older specimens.

All limbs should be fully functional and not swollen. When the chelonian is lifted, do its legs dangle limply from the shell or are they easily straightened when gently pulled? A yes answer to either question likely indicates a problem—possibly malnutrition. Advanced problems can vary from difficult to impossible to correct. Do not purchase the specimen.

Shell

Does the shell have cracks, breaks, missing scutes, or is it pitted? At best your answers will be no, no, no, and no. But some chelonians do experience the trauma of shell breaks or forest fires in the wild. Cracks and breaks can occur and heal satisfactorily, resulting only in cosmetic disfigurement once completely healed.

Burns that have resulted in the loss of scutes may heal and scar—again only a cosmetic problem. If the animal is otherwise healthy and you do not mind the unnatural appearance, there is no reason that you should not purchase it.

While pitting may result from some natural cause, it is most often seen on captives that have been maintained in unclean or other

CHECKLIST

Cautionary Signs

Do not purchase a turtle or tortoise with the following conditions:
✔ Open, unhealed breaks or cracks in the shell
✔ Pits in its shell that contain a caseous, usually odorous, material
✔ Shell of a hatchling that is not firm; shell of an adult that is not rigid
✔ Listless demeanor
✔ Swollen eyelids
✔ Swollen limbs
✔ Exudate around or beneath the eyes
✔ Bubbles from the nostrils when breathing or exudate around the nostrils
✔ Open-mouth breathing
✔ Swimming with one side higher than the other (if a water species)
✔ Difficulty submerging (if a water species)
✔ Limbs that dangle weakly or are easily straightened when the animal is lifted
✔ Limbs obviously flaccid and thin

unsuitable conditions. Like shell breaks, if the pitting is old and well healed, it should cause no further problems. If the pits are unclean and contain an odorous, caseous (cheeselike) material, the problem is active and the specimen should be avoided.

It is often necessary to play a waiting game when you wish to get a good look at a shy tortoise. These creatures are very adept at retiring into their shell, folding their forelimbs tightly in

Sexual Differences

Although sexual characteristics will be mentioned in the various species accounts, here are a few generalities. All pertain to specimens approaching sexual maturity.

✔ The **plastron** (bottom shell) of the males of some turtle and tortoise species is indented (concave). This appears more frequently on terrestrial turtles and tortoises. The concavity allows the male to initially assume a better breeding stance. The concavity does not occur in many semiaquatic turtles, the breeding postures of which are buoyed by the water.

✔ The **foreclaws** of the males of certain semiaquatic turtles are greatly lengthened. Among the species so adorned are the sliders, cooters, painted turtles, and map turtles.

✔ The **tails** of male turtles and tortoises are longer and thicker than those of the females. The vent opening of a male is also positioned more distally from the rear edge of the plastron than that of the female.

front of their head, and sitting for very long periods without displaying any animation. When they finally decide to check things out, they often do so by relaxing the forelimbs somewhat, peering out from between folded elbows, and withdrawing again at the slightest motion. Attempting to check a recalcitrant tortoise can be a true exercise in futility.

Troublesome Developments

If, after getting a chelonian home, it develops troublesome symptoms, consult a veterinarian who is qualified to treat reptile/amphibian ailments and diseases.

Respiratory disease can be communicable and can be caused by a number of different pathogens. Not all of the pathogens respond to the same antibiotics. Isolate any turtle or tortoise that shows symptoms of respiratory distress and have sensitivity tests performed.

Eating

Ask to see the animal eat. Most healthy chelonians have fine appetites. A few specimens may outwardly appear healthy but refuse to feed. Often this lack of appetite results from either illness or an improper diet. It is always a good idea to see the animal feed.

Most aquatic turtles prefer to feed in the water. Some well-acclimated specimens will accept food while out of the water, but will nearly invariably return to the water to consume their morsels. Swallowing is eased by the presence of water in the turtle's mouth and throat. Some hobbyists feel that many aquatic turtle species are unable to swallow unless they are underwater. Although many specimens can and do eat when out of water, most prefer to feed while in water.

Male or Female?

Truthfully, unless you intend to breed your turtles and tortoises, the sex of a specimen is unimportant. Both males and females of most species make equally good pets. The males of some species are larger than the females. In other cases either the opposite is true or both sexes attain a similar size.

Even if it does make a difference, it is nearly impossible to accurately sex hatchling and juvenile turtles and tortoises. It is only when the animals are approaching sexual maturity that the secondary characteristics that allow us to sex them by sight become obvious.

Pet Sources

There are many sources from which you may get a turtle or tortoise. You may choose to collect your own from the wild. Before doing so, check with the landowner if necessary and be sure to check your state's game and nongame laws. Many turtles are protected, some in all states in which they range, some only in the states where they are most uncommon. You may need authorization to collect or keep a native turtle or tortoise, or you may not be legally able to do so at all. Some endangered and threatened species require specific permits. Failure to obtain the permits is a serious offense.

Pet Shops

Many pet shops carry the more commonly available kinds of turtles and tortoises. Should you choose this avenue of acquisition and are not an experienced hobbyist, bring a knowledgeable person with you to help you assess the overall health of the specimen in which you are interested.

Reptile Dealers

Specialty reptile dealers and turtle and tortoise breeders advertise regularly in the classified sections of hobbyist-oriented reptile and amphibian magazines and online. Most are honest and try to supply healthy specimens of high quality; some are unscrupulous. Check the reliability of a given company or person with fellow hobbyists. Since in most cases you will be purchasing the specimen without inspection or appraisal, it is a case of buyer beware. Ask pertinent and pointed questions about the appearance, health, and general hardiness of the specimen and species in question. Be aware that shipping charges

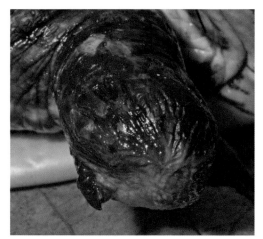

Traumatized limbs will often heal, but there is no appendage regeneration.

(including COD fees if applicable) significantly increase the purchase price.

Health Issues

Whether the initial cost of a turtle or tortoise is small or great, your pet deserves the very best care that can be provided throughout its life. This includes veterinary observation when needed. Your turtle or tortoise did not ask to be taken from the wild; the owning of one is a responsibility that should not be taken lightly.

By providing your turtle or tortoise with a suitable regimen—cleanliness, healthy diet, and a warm, stress-free environment—you can minimize the potential for health problems, but you can never eradicate the possibility of sickness.

Assorted Maladies

As you would with any other pet, find a veterinarian who is qualified to offer care and treatment to your chelonian. Reptilian veterinary medicine is a specialized field. Not all veterinarians choose, or are qualified, to provide treatment to turtles or tortoises. You should find someone qualified before the need arises. That said, let's look at a few of the problems that you may encounter.

Fungal Infections

Aquatic turtles may develop fuzzy gray and white patches that are actually fungal growths. Soft-shelled turtles are especially prone to this problem, and poor water quality is a major cause. Acriflavin or methylene blue, both readily available in aquarium and pet stores, will often eradicate fungal infections when added to the water. If the growths persist, consult a veterinarian.

Swollen Eyelids and Peeling Skin

Acute vitamin A deficiency causes swollen eyelids, which result in vision problems as well as flaking, peeling, and often bloody skin patches.

Although acute vitamin A deficiency is not often encountered, it occurs most commonly in rapidly growing hatchling and juvenile specimens that have had their usually incorrect diets supplemented with only D_3/calcium additives.

Injectable vitamin A may reverse the problem and a better, more balanced diet and multivitamins (rather than just D_3) will prevent its reoccurrence.

Several things other than vitamin A deficiency can cause swollen eyelids and impaired vision in turtles and tortoises. Among other causes are insufficient humidity, old age, advanced systemic disease, and improper diet. A treatment of topical and/or systemic antibiotics is mandatory. Consult your veterinarian.

Obesity

This is as dangerous to turtles and tortoises as to any other animals. In cases of gross obesity, the functions of the liver and other organs are impaired. Correcting the diet in both quality and quantity is recommended.

Respiratory Disease

Clogged or runny nostrils, gasping with open mouth and wheezing, inability to submerge (aquatic species), excessive mucus in the nose and mouth, and bubbling or foaming at the nose and/or mouth indicate serious respiratory problems. The causes can be numerous, singly or in combination.

Respiratory disease can be lingering or rapidly fatal. Antibiotic treatment is mandatory but may differ according to the causative agent. Make your pet comfortable by making sure that the cage is warm enough, or that the patient is utilizing the hot-spot, and consult your veterinarian immediately!

Ear Infections

Ear infections, usually abscesses, resulting from overheating and a humidity too low for the species involved, are not uncommon in ter-

The white-lipped mud turtle, **Kinosternon leucostomum,** *is subtly but attractively colored.*

restrial chelonians, and are quite common in box turtles. We have seen abscesses more rarely on aquatic turtles; poor water quality is most usually the cause in these cases.

Reptilian abscesses do not respond positively to systemic treatments. The abscesses should be surgically removed by a veterinarian. Once the caseous material is removed, the site must be cleaned and bandaged daily. The flushing and dressing is often a simple matter that can be performed at home, but on strong chelonians that remain withdrawn for long periods, veterinary help may continue to be needed.

Mouth Infections

Mouth infections may vary from abscesses to acute infectious stomatitis—literally an infection of the stoma (mouth); also called mouthrot. Abscesses should be surgically removed. Determining what antibiotic to use

against the pathogen will require sensitivity tests. Stomatitis can be fatal; it can quickly progress from tissue to bone structure. If it progresses to the tissues surrounding the trachea, the chelonian may suffocate. In all cases consult your veterinarian.

Shell Problems

Usually of bacterial origin, certain fungi may also be implicated in shell-rot, or **ulcerative shell disease**. Injuries, including burns, bruises, and abrasions that cause breaks in the shell surface, coupled with unsatisfactory hygiene, provide footholds for this disease. Most bacteria implicated are gram-negative varieties. The causative agents must be defined and treated with appropriate antiseptics or antibiotics. While combating this problem, complete sterilization of the quarters, from substrate to heaters, must be done daily. In severely active

This is a hatchling loggerhead musk turtle, **Sternotherus m. minor.**

cases, surgical removal of infected shell areas may be necessary. Untreated cases can be fatal. Consult your veterinarian immediately.

Shell breaks/injuries: Depending on the severity, taping (minor injuries), flushing with antibiotic treatment, and debridement of fragmented shell pieces will be necessary. Fiberglass

TIP

Ask Questions

Do not expect every specimen, especially wild-collected ones, to look picture-book perfect. Turtles and tortoises may vary widely in ground color, markings, and even adult size. The time to ask questions is before the purchase, not after. Good luck!

reconstruction may also be an option. Consult your veterinarian immediately.

Parasites

Terrestrial chelonians collected from the wild may have **ticks, leeches, and bot fly larvae.** Ticks may be removed, after they have been relaxed with a drop of rubbing alcohol or mineral oil, by grasping them and pulling gently, but firmly. Be certain the embedded mouth parts are removed.

Leeches may be found on newly collected aquatic turtles or terrestrial tropical species. A dab of salt on the leech will cause it to loosen its grip and it can then be removed with forceps or fingers.

Certain parasitic flies may lay their eggs on the soft areas of a chelonian's skin. The larvae hatch and burrow beneath the skin. These should be surgically removed by a veterinarian

The plastron (bottom shell) of many hatchling loggerhead musks is brightly colored. Note also that the plastron is of comparatively small size.

as quickly as they are noticed. Bathe the incised area with antiseptics.

Over the course of their lives, many chelonians—even those that are captive-bred and hatched—may be found to have internal parasites. An occasional fecal float and/or mucus swab can determine whether parasites are present. If present, to be effectively purged, these parasites must be properly identified. Because of the complexities of identification of endoparasites, the necessity to accurately weigh specimens to be treated, and the need to measure purge dosages, the eradication of internal parasites is best left to a qualified reptile veterinarian.

Other maladies—from arthritic problems and broken bones to complex infections—are known to afflict chelonians. Veterinary consultation, assessment, and treatment are necessary for most of these problems.

Breeding Concerns

While casual hobbyists may be content merely to keep a turtle or two healthy over the years, many enthusiasts progress well beyond that stage.

As the wild populations diminish, if we hope to continue to have many of our shelled friends available to us as pets for many more years, we must do all possible to keep captive populations stable or increasing through captive breeding efforts.

Over the years, cheloniophiles have learned how to breed many kinds of turtles and tortoises. Suggestions for various species are in the individual species accounts. But here we would like to familiarize you with some of the generalities.

Basics

Except for the Asian big-headed turtle, which occasionally bears live young, all turtles and tortoises reproduce by means of eggs that must be laid on land. Even when conditions are ideal, not all eggs are fertile; mature females can and often do lay clutches of perfectly formed but infertile eggs. Females are also capable of "sperm storage," laying several clutches of fertile eggs after a single mating.

Following copulation, the first clutch of eggs may be laid in three to six weeks. Many species of turtles and tortoises "multi-clutch" annually—that is they lay more than a single clutch of eggs each year. How long it takes for the eggs to hatch is dictated by species and by nest temperature and humidity.

Starting the hatchlings: Assisted by some biodegrading of the shell, the hatchlings cut their way free of the egg with an "egg tooth" or caruncle (this tooth drops off in a few days). It may take a day or longer for the hatchling to finally emerge from the egg. When they emerge from their eggs, hatchling chelonians usually have large umbilical egg sacs. These are absorbed in several hours to about two days. The hatchlings will not need, or even want, to feed until the egg sac has been fully utilized.

Hatchling chelonians, like the young of any living creature, are delicate. Take care that the babies are not on a substrate sufficiently abrasive to rupture the yolk sac. We often keep our hatchlings on dampened paper towels inside their own terrarium until the yolk sac has been absorbed.

We assure all hatchlings with even warmth for the first few weeks of their life. Once the sac is gone, we provide them with large amounts of suitable food. Hatchling tortoises are provided with daily drinking water; hatchling aquatic and semiaquatics are provided with clean water of sufficient depth to enable them to swim. Haul-out areas are nonabrasive and very accessible. Floating plants or other such cover are provided.

The hatchlings of some semiterrestrials (such as wood and bog turtles) often do best if kept for the first few weeks in a small flat container containing about one-quarter inch (.6 cm) of warm water and provided with a hiding area.

The hiding area can be an artificial "cave"; if unmilled sphagnum moss is provided, the turtles make their own hiding area.

Protect hatchlings from predators and overheating if they are taken outside. Remember that jays, crows, and grackles are as avid predators as raccoons, and unfiltered sunlight can overheat a small container to a lethal temperature in a very short time.

Diapause

Excessive heat, cold, moisture, or dryness can kill or deform the embryo. The eggs of many species of turtles and tortoises undergo a diapause—a cessation of embryonic development—for a varying period of time. The diapause may last from only a few days to several weeks. The diapause is often triggered by incubation conditions (such as moisture and temperature) that differ in some way from optimum, but which are actually necessary to embryonic development. In the wild, this may help ensure that the young are hatched at an optimal time for survival.

Reproductive Cycling

The breeding sequences of turtles and tortoises in the wild are triggered largely by external stimuli. Photoperiods, seasonal weather changes (whether these are the traditional annual progression of the seasons of the temperate world or merely the change from dry to rainy season in the tropical areas), hibernation (when applicable), changing barometric pressure, and temperature all contribute significantly to the breeding readiness of most species. Indispensable with all of these, of course, is the coming together of the two sexes at the proper times.

Males of the Aldabra tortoise, Aldabrachelys gigantea, *may exceed 500 pounds (312 kg) in weight.*

The reproductive sequences of temperate turtle and tortoise species are controlled by all five of the above factors. Those of tropical species are controlled by the dry-to-rainy seasonal changes, fluctuations in barometric pressure (low pressures, such as those accompanying the passage of a frontal system or a typhoon often induce breeding behavior), and the encountering of a sexually receptive mate.

It may be necessary to reproduce some or all of these conditions to induce breeding. Even then, our efforts may fail.

Finding a Mate

How do solitary turtles and tortoises find a receptive mate? In their favor is the fact that chelonians are creatures of habit and have a tremendously well-developed homing instinct. They can wander far on land or in water and unerringly return to the tiny area where they hatched. In many cases these treks, or at least the destination of the trek, will bring a given chelonian into contact with others of its own kind. Turtles and tortoises also have remarkable visual acuity. They can probably see other turtles as readily as they see predators.

TIP

Keep Your Eye on the Female

If your turtle or tortoise enclosure is outside, keep an eye on the female as she prepares the nesting site. Crows, magpies, and bluejays watch a nesting female and summon others of their kind. They steal and eat the eggs as they are laid. If you are in an area with fire ants, do not let the eggs hatch in the ground. The ants will find and eat the hatching young.

Certainly not colorful, adult yellow-footed tortoises are personable and hardy.

Pheromones: Many chelonians produce pheromones, scented hormones relating to reproduction. Since the producing glands enlarge during periods of reproductive activity, it is surmised that the pheromone output is greater, and may be scented somewhat differently. Certainly terrestrial species can trail each other for long distances by homing in on the pheromones. The role of pheromone dispersal is less well understood with aquatic species.

Courtship and Copulation

Aquatic and semiaquatic turtles breed while in the water. Some of the courtships, also performed in the water, are intricate and prolonged. Sexually mature males of many species of slider and painted turtles develop greatly lengthened foreclaws that are vibrated and used for stroking the face, neck, and forelimbs of receptive females while the pair is hovering in mid-water. Other species of aquatic or semi-aquatic turtles indulge in stylized vertical head nods or lateral waves of the head and neck while the pair is submerged.

Some species of terrestrial and semiterrestrial turtles may indulge in courtship and breed while on land. Other species may begin courtship on land but breed in the water. A few species, terrestrial throughout most of the year, may seek the water for hibernation and accomplish courtship and breeding just before or after hibernation.

Tortoises court and breed while on land. The courtship of many terrestrial turtles and tortoises is harsh, involving rendering the female immobile by biting or nipping at her head, neck, limbs, and anterior carapace and/or ramming her carapace with that of the male whose head is withdrawn during the procedure. Copulation may be accompanied by shell bumping, biting at the back of the female's head or neck if she extends them, or by head nods and gruff vocalizations (squeals, chuckles, or grunts) by the male.

Nesting Area

No matter whether the species is aquatic, semiaquatic, or terrestrial, you must provide a suitable earthen nesting area. Chelonians that are well acclimated will most often nest as naturally as they would in the wild.

In rare cases the female may simply lay her small clutch atop a protected grass mound or under loose leaf litter. However, most females actually dig a well-defined nest, to whatever depth they are able to reach with their hind legs.

The nesting soil must be deep enough to accommodate the efforts of the female. The soil should be barely dampened so it holds its shape as it is being dug. Collapsing sides or insufficient depth of nesting medium may force the female to discontinue her nesting attempt. The females of a very few species may initially shove dirt or debris aside with the front of the plastron, creating a broad, shallow depression. After completing this to their satisfaction, they will then pivot and dig with their rear legs. According to the species, the nest may be tapered, flasked, or straight-sided.

As she digs, the female turtle or tortoise may moisten the soil with water from her bladder. As the eggs are laid, the female reaches down into the pit with a hind foot and positions each egg. The descent of the dropping eggs may be slowed somewhat by the expulsion of a thick, viscous fluid from the female's vent. Once the clutch is completed, the female covers the nest with the loosened soil and methodically tamps down the covering.

Hibernation

The importance of hibernation to chelonians physiologically adapted to hibernate is largely unknown. (See pages 26–29). Certainly temperate turtles can be kept, and even bred for a few years, without being hibernated. This has been amply proven by breeding successes with wood turtles and Hermann's tortoises kept in outside facilities in southern Florida. However, many breeders have reported a decline in the viability of eggs laid after a few years of nonhibernation by their wood turtles. Since there are no properly hibernated control specimens available for comparison, it is unknown whether the lack of a hibernation period or some other factor is at fault.

The behavior of turtles and tortoises is affected by a variety of external stimuli. These, in turn, stimulate chelonians to hibernate, estivate, and reproduce. Because turtles are poikilothermic (cold-blooded), ambient temperature plays a big part in their overall activity patterns. But seasonal factors such as photoperiod and barometric pressure also influence chelonian activities.

Seasonal "Slowing"

Although tropical species of chelonians may become dormant for short periods of time (triggered by excessive drought or heat), these species are not physiologically programmed to hibernate or estivate (brumate).

On the other hand, even where temperatures do not become prohibitively cold, temperate turtle and tortoise species slow their activities and may actually hibernate for 30, 60, or even 90 days. In this case, it would seem that the cessation of activity is caused more (or at least as much) by waning day lengths than by lowered ambient temperatures.

Whether tropical or temperate in origin, captive chelonians can be induced to remain active year-round by creating artificially long day lengths with electric bulbs and by keeping the animals warm. That the turtles know something is amiss is often attested by diminished appetites and inordinate lethargy during the months they would normally be resting.

Is denial of hibernation healthy for them? We simply don't know—at least we don't know over the long run. We do know that after a few years a chelonian denied hibernation seems to produce larger numbers of inviable eggs. We have also found that, even with suitable warmth, many temperate turtles seem to be more susceptible to respiratory ailments when kept active during the months of winter. We prefer to hibernate our own chelonians that would normally do so in the wild and that are healthy enough to withstand the procedure.

Precautions

Hibernation is not necessarily stress-free for chelonians, whether in the wild or in captivity. Death is far from a stranger at these times. If your turtle or tortoise is not in A-1 condition, do not hibernate it.

And you must know where your specimen originated. It may be that not all populations of a given species hibernate; for instance, spotted turtles from Massachusetts certainly hibernate each winter. Spotted turtles from Florida don't need to hibernate, although they may enter into brief periods of wintertime dormancy.

For semiterrestrial turtles or tortoises, hibernation can be accomplished in two ways—"natural" (on their own) and "artificial" (with a little help from you), but we recommend only the artificial way for aquatic species. Because of the probability of fluctuating temperatures, the natural way is more of a gamble for tortoises as well. If you do intend to hibernate your specimens, make sure they are heavy (but not overtly fat), parasite free, have no signs of respiratory distress, and do not exhibit any other signs of illness or disease.

The Hibernaculum

When you hibernate your chelonian, place it within a hibernation chamber or hibernaculum and place the hibernaculum in a cool area for several weeks. The ideal hibernation temperature—the range you will be striving for—varies from 38 to 45°F (3.3–7.2°C). The humidity of the hibernaculum will vary by species, being higher for aquatic and semiaquatic species than for

This yellow-rimmed box turtle is emerging from the leaf-covered depression where it spent the months of winter.

The Ouachita map turtle, **Graptemys o. ouachitensis,** *is another of the species commonly seen in the pet trade.*

aridland forms. The hibernation period ranges from as few as 60 to as many as 120 days.

Before Hibernation

One of the most critical factors is actually a prehibernation concern. A turtle's or tortoise's gut must be empty of food before the animal is hibernated. A chelonian's rate of digestion varies with ambient temperature. Warm days and warm nights promote rapid digestion. Warm days and cool nights favor slower digestion, and cool days and cool nights make for very slow digestion.

Thus, you must know your animal and stop feeding it from two weeks (warm areas) to four weeks (cool areas) before it is allowed to hibernate. An occasional soak in warm water may hasten defecation. Err on the side of safety. Continue to provide water throughout the prehibernation fast.

Natural Hibernation

If you live in a temperate area and keep your turtles or tortoises outdoors the most likely candidates for natural hibernation are Eastern, three-toed, ornate, and desert box turtles and Hermann's and Central Asian tortoises. These chelonians all naturally hibernate on land and are quite adept at finding suitable niches, even in captivity.

Just make sure that they dig well below the frost line. Many hobbyists in the northern United States add a 1 foot (30 cm) cover of fallen leaves after the chelonians have dug in and have entered dormancy. Do make certain that the turtles/tortoises have not dug into a floodprone area. Make sure the area is fenced, or that the hibernaculum is covered with wire netting. Remember also that predators, such as domestic dogs, raccoons, and bears, will dine on hibernating turtles if the opportunity presents itself. Use necessary precautions.

Bog turtles, **Glyptemys muhlenbergi,** *are characterized by the orange head markings.*

Fire ants: Fire ants, now commonplace throughout the Gulf states and westward to California, prey on ground nesting animals such as turtles and tortoises.

Shrews: Shrews, with their digging skills, acute smelling ability, and prodigious appetites, can make quick work of a hibernating turtle or tortoise.

Warm periods: Watch that the chelonians do not emerge from hibernation during any unnaturally warm periods. If they do, they should be brought indoors to finish their hibernation cycle or be warmed and fed from that point on.

If at any time you are able to tell that a chelonian has urinated during its dormancy, it is best to rouse the specimen and let it drink before either continuing hibernation or warming it for the remainder of the season.

Artificial Hibernation

Artificial hibernation may be arranged in several ways. Because we live in a mild climate, we have found that the best method for us involves using a modified refrigerator.

Each aquatic and semiterrestrial turtle is placed in an individual plastic box that is filled with moist, unmilled sphagnum moss. The turtles, boxes, and all, are then placed in a refrigerator modified to retain temperatures between 40 and 44°F (4.4–6.6°C). The turtles are checked periodically and are roused for the duration should we feel all is not well, such as slight weight, sunken eyes, or poor respirations.

The hibernating tortoises are housed in the same cooling unit, but are in deeper plastic boxes filled with dried leaves or dry sphagnum. The condition of each tortoise is checked at two-week intervals. Again, should we feel a problem

Despite the bright colors, the pattern of the star tortoise camouflages it well in areas of dappled sunlight.

exists (it seldom does) the tortoise is roused, warmed, and kept active for the duration.

In cooler areas, turtles and tortoises are often hibernated in root cellars or other such underground "steady temperature" storage areas that retain cool temperatures of 35 to 45°F (1.6–7.2°C).

In these areas tortoises are hibernated using two boxes, one inside the other with insulating material between (Styrofoam peanuts are ideal). The inner box contains the tortoise and leaves or other basically inert material that is not prone to mildew or mold. Neither straw nor hay is recommended for use either in the inner box

or between the two boxes. Keep an eye on temperatures. Even with heavy insulation, sustained temperatures below freezing will prove devastating or fatal to the turtle or tortoise. The temperature inside the hibernaculum should be from 40 to 44°F (4.4–6.6°C).

At the End of the Hibernation Period

When ground temperatures naturally warm, those turtles or tortoises that are hibernating naturally will simply wake up and dig themselves out. For those that you are hibernating, simply bring the hibernaculum to normal room temperature and allow the chelonians to awaken.

If we are present as the eggs are being laid, we remove them once they emerge from the mother. To do this we merely scoop out the back side of the hole so that we may maneuver without bumping the female. If we are not present, we carefully dig up the eggs at our earliest convenience, and place them in small plastic containers half-filled with dampened vermiculite; the containers are then put into the incubator.

Egg Orientation

After incubation has begun, it is important that the eggs not be rotated on either longitudinal axis. To help us with egg orientation, we pencil a small "X" on the top of each egg before it is moved. Reptile eggs, unlike bird eggs, do not require turning during incubation (nor once incubating can reptile eggs survive turning through the end of the second trimester). They are able to survive some turning during the final trimester, but there is no reason to do so.

Incubation

Chelonian eggs require warmth—77 to 86°F (25–30°C)—and moisture to develop. During the summer, the eggs of temperate species of turtle/tortoises will usually develop satisfactorily at high normal room temperature –77 to 80°F (25–26.6°C).

Tropical species, or species from warmer microhabitats in temperate areas of either the southern or northern hemisphere (deserts, etc.), will need to be kept a little warmer than normal room temperatures—80 to 86°F (26.6–30°C). We keep our incubators set at 84 to 86°F (28.8–30°C), a range satisfactory for most tropical species, but the eggs of red-footed and yellow-footed tortoises would develop more reliably at between 78 and 82°F (25.5–27.7°C).

Vermiculite

It seems as if each hobbyist has a preferred way of incubating eggs. Among other mediums, substrates of torn newspaper, perlite, soil, sand, and vermiculite have been suggested. We prefer vermiculite. The amount of water we mix with the vermiculite varies by species. The eggs of rain forest tortoises and aquatic turtles, for example, require a greater amount of moisture than the eggs of arid-land or desert species.

To moisten the vermiculite, add water and mix until the vermiculite clumps together when squeezed in your hand. The volumes will be about four parts vermiculite to one part water, but add that water sparingly; you may need less. When the mixture clumps

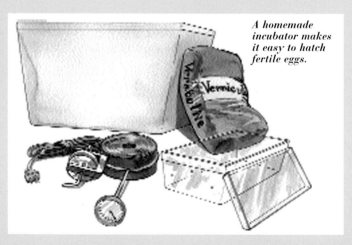

A homemade incubator makes it easy to hatch fertile eggs.

when squeezed, that's the consistency to use for forestland species.

For desert species, squeeze the vermiculite until you squeeze out a little of the water, or use less water to start with. One third to one half of the height of the egg should be nestled into the vermiculite.

If we choose to retain a high relative humidity for some of the eggs, the dampened vermiculite and eggs are placed in small covered containers inside the incubator. It is usually best to leave the top off the small containers that hold the eggs of arid-land species. In both cases, we place an open Styrofoam cup of water in the bottom of the incubator. If it becomes necessary to remoisten the substrate, take care not to wet the eggs.

Hatchlings

The hatchlings may remain in the egg for a day or even longer after pipping has occurred. This is normal and their removal from the egg should not be hastened. In most cases, the hatchlings are still resorbing the yolk sac, and will have difficulty walking or swimming if they are physically removed.

However, if after two or three days the hatchling has still not fully emerged, it is probably best to assist it. To do this, enlarge the break in the eggshell that the hatchling initially made so that the baby turtle/tortoise can be easily slipped from the egg. Use extreme care not to break the yolk sac if any remains unresorbed. Place the hatchling on a dampened paper towel in a shallow receptacle from which it cannot escape. Keep the paper towel moistened until the yolk sac is completely resorbed and the umbilical opening is mostly (or fully) closed.

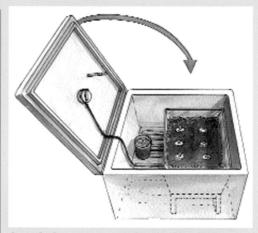

Once the heat tape is wired to the thermostat and the unit plugged in, you can add the container of eggs.

At that time the baby may be treated like any other baby turtle or tortoise. If it is an aquatic species, it may be placed in shallow water for its first swim. If it is a terrestrial species, it can be kept on a smooth substrate for another few days, but it can eventually be placed on whatever substrate you normally use for other baby turtles.

Continuing to utilize the food energy from its yolk sac, the baby will not eat for a few days after hatching. Again, this is normal. However, within a few days, the hatchling will begin searching for food and should be eating heartily soon thereafter. Aquatic species should be fed in the water and, of course, hatchlings of terrestrial species should be fed on the land. Be certain that the food items offered are small enough for the babies to easily grasp and swallow and that the food is of a healthy, nourishing variety. Provide vitamin D_3-calcium supplements at this time to assure the normal growth and development of the baby.

CARING FOR YOUR PET

Once you decide on what type of turtle or tortoise you want, you'll have to focus on what type of housing you need to provide.

There are several easily set up and easily maintained caging types, depending on the type of turtle or tortoise you are keeping and your own needs.

Housing Needs for Turtles

Most turtles need to be either in water or close to it, but some types, such as the wood turtle or the box turtle, are more terrestrial than aquatic. Whatever kind of turtle you have, remember to add a lamp or hot-spot (an incandescent bulb, usually 75 watts or more, which emits heat and light) over the basking area.

Aquatic Turtles

Indoor caging: You'll need an aquarium (remember, aquatic turtles are active, so the larger the tank, the better), 1 inch (2.5 cm) or

A desert box turtle hatchling, **Terrapene ornata luteola.**

so of river rock or gravel on the bottom, and a filter system. Filtration can be undergravel or via an outside filter.

If you use an undergravel filter, attach a powerhead pump or a small vibratortype aerating pump to the upright filter tube. The powerhead pump provides a fairly strong water current that pulls down and filters the water through the gravel and then pushes the water out the top of the powerhead. The small vibrator-type pump does the same with reduced power by using air bubbles to push water through the upright filter tube. Keep in mind that some turtles are weak swimmers or small turtles may not be able to negotiate the strong current caused by the powerhead.

Add large smooth rocks or semisubmerged logs for a haul-out area under the tank's light or hot-spot. Your basking turtles, the sliders and cooters, will avail themselves of a dry haul-out and spend a good part of the day sunning. If you have tiny hatchling turtles that you've caught yourself (you cannot legally buy any turtles that are less than 4 inches (10 cm) long, because of *Salmonella* concerns), a good-sized patch of floating aquatic plants will work for a resting/sunning area. Musk and soft-shelled turtles will rest atop these floating plants, rather than on a log or rock.

Place the tank on a sturdy tabletop or on a stand and pour in the rinsed river rock or gravel. Spread the rock or gravel evenly. We prefer river rock because the stones are rounded (not sharp like aquarium gravel) and of a size that cannot be swallowed by the turtles. Turtles routinely search along the bottom of their tank and ingest gravel as part of the feed/exploration process. If too much sharp gravel is ingested, intestinal impaction can occur.

Add water to about half the depth of the tank. If you're keeping soft-shelled turtles, you may want to add a dechlorinator to remove the chlorine from the water. Soft-shelled turtles have a leathery, soft shell rather than the hard

shells of most turtles, and so are more subject to shell damage and fungus problems (especially as babies—and most especially, the babies of the Florida soft-shelled turtle, Trionyx ferox). A fine sand substrate will help them keep their shell clean and healthy.

Plants: Almost any type of aquatic plant can be used in your tank. Plants add to the appearance; turtles may use them as resting areas and munch on them as well. Plants netted from the wild may bear the additional bonus of tiny succulent insects and snails. Be prepared to add more plants as the old ones are eaten. You'll need to replant them in the tank when they are uprooted by the turtles. Place your plants, rocks, and logs to advantage.

Water level: Being air-breathers, of course, turtles need to be able to stick their noses above the surface of the water. A lower water level—one about 5 inches (12.5 cm) or less—means the turtles can draw a fresh breath of air while standing on their toes on the bottom of the tank and extending their necks. A lower water level also makes it easier for the turtles to crawl out on their haul-out areas to dry off, and eliminates the possibility of their getting too close to the overhead light or crawling out of the tank altogether. If you want to fill your tank nearer to the top, be certain that there are floating logs so your turtles can crawl out, dry off, and sun themselves under the aquarium light.

Semiterrestrial Turtles

Turtles that are well adapted to spending part of their life on land are called semiterrestrial turtles. Two examples are wood turtles and

*This Brazilian slider, **Trachemys dorbignyi**, is at home in a garden pond.*

The Burmese star tortoise, **Geochelone platynota,** *is an endangered species.*

box turtles. Enclosures for the semiterrestrials need more land than water. The land base is created by placing 1 to 2 inches (2.5–5 cm) of river gravel in the bottom of a tank, placing a layer of nylon netting or air conditioner filtering material atop the gravel, and then adding 1 to 2 inches (2.5–5 cm) of potting soil on top. The netting or filtration material prevents the topsoil from shifting into the gravel, while the gravel serves as a drainage reservoir that keeps the topsoil damp without becoming soggy.

Water dish: Water for these terrestrials can be provided in a dish that is firmly anchored in the substrate. The dish needs to be large enough for a turtle to drink from and crawl into, but not so deep that the turtle cannot easily crawl out of it. This water will need to be kept clean by frequent changes; although semi-terrestrial turtles do not need to defecate into water, many seem to prefer it. The water will also get dirty from the bits of soil clinging to the turtle's face or shell. Changing the water three or four times a week should be sufficient.

Hiding place: Like the aquatic turtles, the semiterrestrial turtles will be more comfortable if they have a hiding place. This can be a box with an entry hole, a piece of flat bark placed over the rims of two adjacent small pots of plants, or any other type of enclosing space. However, some specimens may merely wedge themselves tightly into a corner of the enclosure, using this in preference to the enclosure you have provided. Many terrestrial turtles (and tortoises, too) will return to the same spot each night to sleep.

Decorations: The enclosure for the wood and box turtles lends itself well to additional decoration in the form of plants or artistically

Backyard turtle ponds may be constructed from many materials and in shapes to fit in any open, sunny space.

shaped logs. Plants can stay in their pots and simply be embedded in the substrate up to the pot rims. (Since semiterrestrial turtles are, by nature, rather like small bulldozers, the plants used should be sturdy, nontoxic if nibbled, able to withstand substantial abuse, and/or readily replaced.) Vines, like philodendron, lend themselves to this sort of tank, and their stems provide more exploration areas for the turtles. The semiterrestrial turtles, which tend to be more adventuresome and active than either the wholly aquatic turtles or the tortoises, will investigate any new addition to their enclosure.

Housing for Tortoises

Tortoises need almost the same type of enclosure as the semiterrestrials, but prefer even drier conditions. Substrate for them can be dry river rock, newspaper, mulch, pieces of indoor-outdoor carpeting cut to the size of the enclosure, or the tiny compressed alfalfa pellets used as rabbit food. Each type of substrate, of course, has its advantages and disadvantages.

River rock is easy to wash when dirty and provides traction that makes walking easy. Newspaper is readily available, absorbent, and

easily changed, but its smooth surface makes walking uncomfortable, if not actually difficult, for some tortoises. We use newspaper only short-term, such as during transport. Cypress or pine mulch (never cedar; it contains phenols that are harmful to skin and lungs of reptiles) provides good footing and is absorbent but may cause impactions if ingested. Indoor-outdoor carpeting also provides a secure walking surface and can be washed or discarded when it becomes dirty.

Pelleted alfalfa is dry, inexpensive, and provides traction, and if it's accidentally ingested while the tortoise is feeding, no harm is done. However, since the pellets absorb both moisture and contaminants, the condition of the alfalfa pellets must be carefully monitored.

Water: Provide water in a shallow, untippable container. Stainless steel or heavy ceramic water dishes are both suitable for watering bowls. Small plastic dishes, partially buried in the substrate can be used but then reconcile yourself to straightening and refilling them frequently. It will also be necessary to change wet substrate often to keep it dry.

Wild: In the wild, tortoises have a rather well-defined home range and usually a shelter (of sorts) to which they regularly retire. Captives should have a hiding place much like those provided for semiterrestrial turtles. A cardboard box with an access hole works well, or if you add a few pots of vines and pull some of the twining stems to one side, the tortoise may use the vines as cover.

Algae often grows on the shell of turtles that spend much time in the water. This is an albino red-ear.

amount of water in the pool will heat up quickly.

2. Create sunning areas for the turtles by positioning logs and/or smooth rocks in the center of the pool, and add the water with a garden hose. (You can probably see already how much less work an outdoor enclosure is going to be; cleaning and refilling is easy.)

3. Keep the water level high enough so the turtles can totally submerge, but not so deep that they can lever themselves over the edge of the pool.

4. Add turtles, feed as needed, and clean the pool every couple of days or when needed. You can hose off the algae or wipe the pool down as part of the cleaning process, but don't add any chemicals to kill or inhibit the algae.

The only problem with this type of pool is that it provides no land area for the female to lay her eggs, and eggs laid in water will literally drown.

Aquatic Turtle Pond

If you can devote any type of yard space to the aquatic turtle pond, you can submerge it to its rim in the soil, and add a 1-foot-high (30 cm) fence about 3 feet (91 cm) from the rim of the pond.

Plant shrubs and other types of cover, especially if the pond receives more than a couple of hours of direct sun each day. This will enable your turtles to wander about at will on the dry land, and should a female be carrying eggs, she can easily dig a hole to bury her eggs.

Outdoor Caging

Outdoor caging not only decreases your workload, but provides a better environment for your turtles and tortoises. The length of time during the day/year that your turtles can be kept outside will be determined by both the temperature of the surrounding environment (ambient temperature) and the turtle/tortoise species involved. As may be expected, species from temperate regions can withstand cooler temperatures for longer periods than can tropical forms.

Kiddie Pools

Aquatic turtles do quite well in something as simple as a kiddie wading pool. Buy one without a ramp leading to the rim of the pool, or your turtles may take advantage of the opportunity to do some real traveling.

1. Place the pool in a partially shaded area. The turtles need and enjoy sun, but the small

Laws on Keeping Turtles

Turtles and tortoises under 4 inches (10 cm) in length may be sold only to researchers. Why is this so and how did it come to be?

Well, certainly for humane reasons changes were needed. But it was not the ethics of humane treatment that stopped baby turtle sales. Rather, it was concern about the possible spread of a bacterial disease—salmonellosis (often just referred to by the generic name of the bacterium—*Salmonella*).

Salmonella is an omnipresent bacterium, and improper hygiene in the tanks of baby turtles often assured that it would be present in noteworthy concentrations in those containers.

In the late 1970s, conservationists and health officials combined forces and a federal law was passed preventing the sale of baby turtles—of any turtle (including tortoises)—with a shell length of 4 inches (10 cm) or less. The rationale was that the toddlers for whom the baby turtles were often purchased as pets would be unable to put a turtle of 4-inch (10 cm) or more in their mouths; thus, possible contamination by Salmonella bacteria would be lessened.

The fallacy, of course, is that though the turtles may not fit easily in the mouth, fingers do. If *Salmonella* are present, unwashed hands can easily transmit the bacteria to the mouth.

Thus, the bottom line here is to caution both adults and children: Turtles can carry diseases that are transmissible to humans, and you may inadvertently introduce pathogens to your pets if you handle them or offer them food without first washing your hands. If you wash your hands both before and following the handling of any pet turtles or tortoises, you will help protect both your pets and yourself.

Indigenous and Protected Species

Today, additional laws that affect the availability of turtles and tortoises in the pet trade have also been enacted. Many states now fully or partially protect all or some indigenous turtle species. Endangered species regulations on state, federal, and international levels offer even greater protection to some species. Importation restrictions limit the availability of many foreign turtle species once sought by American hobbyists.

But despite all of the laws and regulations, people continue to keep turtles and tortoises, baby and otherwise. There are many breeders of both common and unusual turtles and tortoises. Baby turtles are found by anglers who take them home to their families, children pick up box and wood turtles on woodland pathways, and reptile dealers can supply a vast number of species. Specialty clubs, catering to cheloniophiles (turtle enthusiasts) are present in many large cities.

Thus, if you want a turtle, you can get a turtle. And if that turtle is cared for properly, it may live for decades.

Bog turtles are now protected. Be certain of the legality of any you intend to purchase.

Garden Pools

Turtle pools need not be merely of the child's wading variety. They may be as elaborate as you wish. A large free-form pool may be provided with a bridge or overhanging platform on which you can sit while watching your turtles. A free-form pond may be of any size you choose and can have either a smooth concrete or a pliable pool liner bottom. A depth of about 18 inches (45 cm) at the deepest point should slope gently upward to only an inch or two (2.5–5 cm) at the shoreline.

Galvanized cattle-watering tanks can also be used. These have diameters of from 2 to 12 feet (61–366 cm). A water depth of about 18 inches (45 cm) should be maintained and some large pieces of driftwood and sunken logs for haulout perches must be provided. Plants may also be grown in these pools but may be consumed by herbivorous turtle species.

Both semiterrestrial turtles and tortoises do well in a fenced enclosure with a sunken water dish. A Pyrex baking dish is sturdy enough to be hosed out or lifted and cleaned and yet shallow enough to allow the turtles to enter and leave at will.

The lid of a trash container, sunk to its rim, may be a more suitable water container for multiple or larger specimens. You need to keep the water container fairly shallow because some of the semiterrestrial turtles, such as the box turtle, do not swim well. A plastic container lid placed on the ground will keep food items out of the dirt.

A hiding area such as a pile of leaf litter, planted shrubs, or a hiding box will provide your turtle or tortoise with a greater feeling of security.

The Enclosed Garden

Although not often used by American hobbyists, the European concept of tortoises and terrestrial turtles wandering free in an enclosed garden or yard does find favor with some. The creatures enjoy the space, are very active, and behave more naturally then when in a small cage. Tortoises will often follow their keepers around like so many well-trained dogs, moving when the keeper moves and gathering around when the keeper stops.

The night house: If you feed the turtles and tortoises in one place and at a particular time, the creatures will often gather daily in anticipation of their meal and they learn equally fast where their night house is. Even in southern Florida it is necessary to heat the night house on some of the colder evenings. This can be accomplished by using red or blue heat lamps,

Radiated tortoises, Geochelone radiata, and endangered species, are prettily colored and of moderate size.

neither of which seemed to disturb the tortoises' 24-hour biological cycle (circadian rhythms) and breeding cycles in the slightest.

Fencing: No matter how tightly a steel-mesh fence is stretched, there is no such thing as tortoise-escape-proof chain-link fencing. Large tortoises can walk right under what seems to be a taut, ground-hugging chain-link fence. Reinforce the bottom of the fencing by securing ground-level rebars (reinforcing bars) parallel to the ground between the fenceposts. An alternative is to run treated 1 × 6s along the bottom of the fence, staking them at 4-foot (1.2 m) intervals. In some areas of the country, cinder block walls are commonly placed around yards and gardens. These are ideal for the chelonians and need no additional preparation at all.

Dietary Requirements

Although many arid-land tortoises metabolize much of their moisture requirements from the food they eat, it is important that all captive chelonians be provided clean water at all times. Tortoises are not nimble creatures. Not only must the water dish be easy to drink from, but it must be shallow enough so the tortoise won't drown if it happens to bumble in and overturn.

Water receptacles may be small enough so that the tortoise/turtle only drinks from it, or large enough to allow your pet to fully enter and soak. Whatever the size, the receptacles must be shallow and they must be kept full. To protect the plastron from abrasion, the sides must be smooth and easily negotiated.

The Thai big head is an aptly named and rather pretty turtle species.

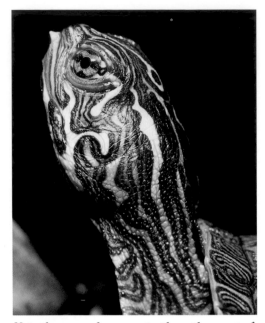

Note the caruncle or egg tooth on the snout of this hatchling northern red-bellied cooter.

Aquatic chelonians will, of course, drink from their swimming water—another reason that filtration and changing is so important. Do note that many aquatic turtle species feed in the water. Depending on the number of turtles kept in any self-contained aquatic enclosure and the gallonage of the enclosure itself, occasional to frequent and partial to complete water changes should be routinely made.

Food Selection

You have one simple goal in feeding your turtle or tortoise: learn what your pet eats in the wild and strive to simulate this. Your pet will be much the better for your efforts.

Here are some general guidelines. For species-specific suggestions, read the species accounts beginning on page 51. Keep in mind that you must stop feeding any chelonians you intend to hibernate two weeks (or more, depending on ambient temperatures) prior to placing them into hibernation. (See pages 25–29 on hibernation.)

Supplementation

In all diets, augment with calcium and multivitamins (specifically D_3 and some A). This is especially important in fast-growing hatchlings and juveniles and in ovulating females, all of which are actively metabolizing calcium.

For all reptiles, a diet with the correct calcium to phosphorus balance is important to maintain bone integrity. If the reptile does not receive enough calcium in its diet to maintain the correct level in the blood, the needed cal-

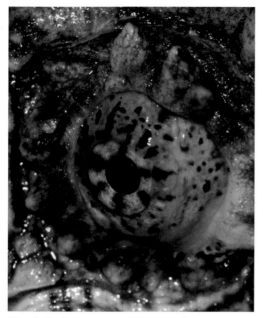

Here's looking at you. The eye of the alligator snapping turtle.

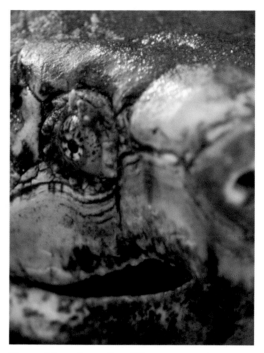

Everything about the alligator snapping turtle, **Macroclemys temminckii,** *looks tough and resilient.*

cium is taken from the bones. The bones are softened and muscles weaken; the syndrome is termed metabolic bone disease, or MBD.

For shelled creatures, the importance of maintaining good bone/shell strength is obvious. All you have to do is provide the foods that enable the chelonian to maintain this balance—and it's not complicated. Avoid feeding exclusively foods that are high in phosphorus and low in calcium. These include grapes, bananas, mealworms, crickets, and fresh peas.

With its oxalic acid content, spinach presents a special problem. This combines with calcium to form an insoluble salt, calcium oxalate, which builds up in the kidneys. Spinach should not be fed to chelonians. The ratio of calcium to phosphorus in the total diet, including supplements,

Fruits and Vegetables with Calcium/Phosphorous Ratio of 1:1 or Better

avocado	cauliflower
beet greens	celery
blackberries	chard
blueberries	collards
broccoli stem or leaf (not florets)	dandelion greens
	endive
cabbage	green beans
Chinese cabbage	kohlrabi
cantaloupe	okra
carrots	

This is a hatchling pastel red-eared slider.

should be a minimum of 2:1. Check the nutrition labels on the containers of packed turtle/tortoise foods and supplements for the proportions of calcium and phosphorous.

Vitamin D$_3$ and calcium: Vitamin D$_3$ assists the proper metabolism of calcium. Most calcium additives designed for reptile consumption now contain D$_3$. Improper metabolism of calcium or actual lack of calcium in the diet can result in soft bones and shell. Make certain that the diet you provide fulfills your chelonian's needs from the start. If you acquire a turtle or tortoise with this deficiency, take the animal to your reptile veterinarian.

Calcium injections can often stabilize or actually reverse the deterioration, and a better, more balanced diet will help prevent reoccurrence. Most turtles and tortoises will quickly develop bad dietary habits if the opportunity is presented. This includes those primarily herbivorous species that are fed more than minimal amounts of animal protein. A high protein diet will often cause improper shell growth as well.

Diet for Aquatic or Semiaquatic Turtles

Although most turtles in these categories consume some aquatic vegetation, most are quite carnivorous, eating aquatic insects, worms, crayfish, and snails. However, the sliders and cooters of the genera *Pseudemys* and *Trachemys* are more herbivorous, grazing extensively on aquatic plants such as *Anacharis, Elodea, Hydrilla,* and the various eelgrasses or turtle grasses. Captives will eat romaine, dandelion leaves and flowers, grated squash, aquarium plants, and other suitable dark, leafy vegetables (see caution regarding spinach, above), as well as grated fruits and some animal protein. Trout, catfish, and cat chows are excellent, and if used in moderation, many of the prepared turtle foods now on the market are satisfactory.

The Thai big-head, **Platysternon megacephalum peguense,** *is now a comparative rarity in the hobby.*

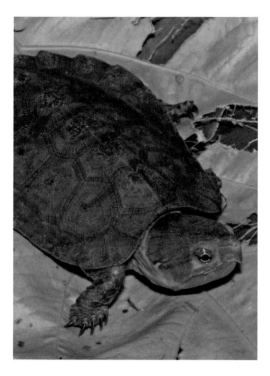

Diet for Terrestrial or Semiterrestrial Turtles

Contrary to popular belief, box turtles, like other terrestrial and semi-terrestrial species, are not exclusively herbivorous or frugivorous. Although they will eat some fruit, the various box turtles eat worms, slugs, snails, insects, and carrion as well. The western box turtles (*Terrapene ornata* ssp.) are preferentially insectivorous. Newly born (pinky) mice will be eagerly accepted by most; many specimens will accept rehydrated trout, catfish, and cat chows. Many of the prepared turtle foods now on the market are excellent supplements.

Diet for Map Turtles

Insects and gastropod mollusks figure prominently in the diet of map turtles in the wild. Insects, worms, and snails are important to captive specimens as well. These turtles eat little vegetation but may pick at romaine and dandelion leaves as well as at aquarium plants. Trout, catfish, and cat chows, used in combination, seemingly form a good base diet for these active turtles.

Diet for Forest and Wooded Savanna Tortoises

Tortoise species such as red-footed, yellow-footed, and hinge-backs require a small to moderate amount of animal protein in their diet. Besides fruits and vegetables, some trout and catfish chow and low-fat cat chows should be provided. Star tortoises, elongated tortoises, and others of similar habits and habitats seem to do best when only small amounts of animal protein are provided.

Diet for Arid-Land Tortoises

The various European tortoises, leopard tortoises, both spur-thighed tortoises, radiated tortoises, and gopher and desert tortoises are predominantly herbivorous. They should be given wellrounded vegetable diets and very little fruit. Among other things we provide romaine, escarole, bok choy, okra, a few green beans, bean sprouts, alfalfa sprouts, rabbit pellets, dandelion leaves and flowers, and grated squash. We provide a very little rehydrated, low-fat cat chow about once a month.

Like almost all turtles, musk and mud turtles will bite painfully if carelessly restrained. This is a Flordia mud turtle, **Kinosternon subrubrum steindachneri.**

How Often Should Food Be Offered?

The intake of food by turtles and tortoises will vary according to their metabolic rate. Being ectotherms, with the body temperature close to that of the environment, the bodily functions of chelonians are more active when they are warm than when they are cold. When a turtle or tortoise becomes too cold, digestion can stop and putrefaction can occur in the gut, causing distress or even death.

Optimum temperatures: For most turtles and tortoises these are between 78 and 90°F (25.5–32.2°C). (For more specific information, see species accounts beginning on page 51.) Even on cooler days, if the sun is shining, the chelonians will bask (thermoregulate) and raise their body temperatures. Aquatic species accomplish this by either hauling out on the bank, clambering up on an exposed snag or rock, or floating at the surface of the water. When it is cool and conditions do not permit thermoregulation, turtles become lethargic and inactive.

When they are at their optimum warmth, turtles and tortoises will eat surprisingly large amounts of food daily. When they are cooler, less food is necessary. When they are cooler yet, such as when you are preparing them for hibernation, food should be withheld entirely (see pages 25–29).

Deprived in captivity of space for normal activity, turtles and tortoises can become unhealthily obese. Many advanced hobbyists use scales to watch the weight of their specimens. Far less sophisticated, our method is to know the specimen. It is not difficult to see signs of weight loss or gain and to alter the dietary offerings accordingly.

Correcting Dietary Mistakes

As mentioned earlier, chelonians can become very fond of, even addicted to, incorrect diets. This is unhealthy and must be altered at the earliest opportunity. If you continue to offer them the dietary items to which they are accustomed, as well as provide the correct new foods, your pets will often resist the change. In most cases, the quickest and best way to effect the change is to withhold the incorrect foods while providing ample amounts of the correct ones. Your turtle or tortoise may rebel by not eating for a day, a week, even a fortnight (or longer), but when sufficiently hungry it will eat.

For the most reluctant specimens, you may wish to smear small amounts of their favored foods on the new kinds. Sometimes just adding the scent of the previous food will facilitate the acceptance of the better food by your shelled pet.

Although this may seem cruel to you, in the long run it is much kinder than subjecting your turtle or tortoise to diet-related maladies such as metabolic bone disease or visceral gout. If you suspect that diet-related health problems are already present, consult your veterinarian.

Prepackaged Options

Prepacked vegetable salad mixtures are available in many stores. You may find purchasing these more suitable than mixing your own tortoise food. There is nothing wrong with this, but we suggest that if spinach is a part of the purchased mixture that all (or at least most) of it be removed. Do not use badly wilted or discolored vegetables.

Prepacked turtle and tortoise foods are also now available. While some of these may be complete diets and suitable for a base diet, we suggest that all be augmented with fresh natural items.

Rather than search for worms every time we need them, we collect all that we can when they are abundant (such as after dark on sidewalks and roads, following a spring or autumn rain) and we set up a worm-holding facility in a cool area. That sure beats hefting a shovel every time a turtle acts hungry.

We also buy crickets and mealworms wholesale. You can often work out a cheaper price with your local pet store or you may choose to buy from a wholesaler. Either way, it will save you money. Wholesalers advertise in the various reptile and amphibian magazines listed in the Information section (page 108).

You'll need to provide a source of heat and light for turtles and tortoises. Like most of us, turtles and tortoises seems to prefer bright light. For them, a bright light activates feeding and other activity responses. Combined light and heat is especially important during the cooler months.

Benefits of Warmth

The light and heat are important because chelonians are dependent on external heat sources; if they can't warm up, body functions (such as digestion) slow or stop. A warm turtle or tortoise

✔ feeds readily
✔ is able to digest its food

✔ is alert enough to respond to your presence.

Depending on its area of origin, a chelonian will be most comfortable when kept between 75 to 85°F (24–29°C), with a hot-spot basking area.

There are a couple of easy ways to heat your chelonian's enclosure. For aquatic turtles, you can use a nonbreakable (titanium) submersible aquarium heater that lies on the bottom of the tank. (With a lowered tank level, the usual hang-over-the-edge heaters cannot be used.) If you choose an in-tank heater, protect it from being banged against the side of the tank by the turtles as they explore and feed.

Undertank Heater

Some people use an electric heating pad underneath the tank. Just be sure that the pad and its wire always are protected from the water in the tank.

An under-tank heater (a specially made heating "pad") will fit underneath an aquatic tank or under a terrarium and cannot be damaged by an active turtle or tortoise.

Illuminated Basking Area

Even if under-tank heaters are used, brilliantly illuminated basking areas will be appreciated by your turtles and tortoises. For an aquatic tank, center the illumination above the haul-out area. Remember that fluorescent fixtures provide light but little heat. We use a 75-watt incandescent bulb in a round metal reflector, suspended over the tank about 12 to 18 inches (30–45 cm) above the basking/haul-out area.

Temperature

Temperature on the basking area should be about 88 to 94°F (31–34°C); the water in the tank must be cooler for thermoregulation.

This type of incandescent light will also work for your

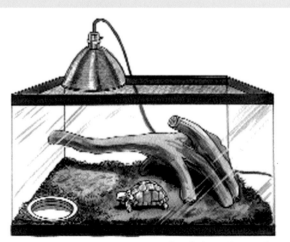

A tortoise terrarium set-up must provide a hiding place, a hot-spot, a feeding area, water, and a substrate that offers walking traction.

tortoises, again centered over the spot in the enclosure that is the hot-spot. For both turtles and tortoises, provide at least six hours of warmth-with-light a day.

Full-Spectrum Incandescent Bulbs

It is now possible to purchase full-spectrum incandescent bulbs that provide beneficial ultraviolet rays (UV-A and UV-B) for the basking turtles. Providing full-spectrum lighting for your pets certainly can't hurt, but the truth seems to be that full-spectrum lighting isn't an absolute necessity when maintaining most chelonians.

However, since UV-A and UVB rays assist reptiles in synthesizing and metabolizing certain vitamins and minerals, if full-spectrum lighting is not utilized, vitamin D_3 and calcium supplements must be provided more regularly.

Overheating: Tortoises and highly domed turtles are not agile, and they may overturn. Once overturned, they may find it difficult or impossible to right themselves. If this occurs in full sunlight or beneath a heat lamp, your pet may overheat and die. Although there is no fail-safe method to prevent this, you must take every precaution possible. Take stock of your caging, redecorate as prudent, and check your chelonian daily.

Consider a Timer

Lighting and heating are both of paramount importance to the well-being of turtles and tortoises. But neither is needed in full intensity around the clock. In fact, providing a day-night (photoperiod-influenced) variation in temperature and lighting can be of more benefit to your tortoise than utilizing either steadily around the clock.

The intent of both heating and lighting is to provide your turtle or tortoise with tempera-

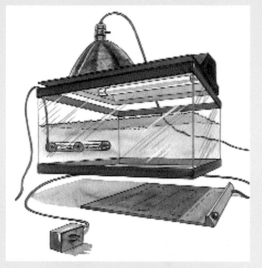

Choose among these techniques to heat an aquatic cage: overhead incandescent light, submerged aquarium heater, or under-tank heating pad. The fluorescent light in the hood provides illumination only; not an appreciable amount of heat.

tures and light intensities that are suitable for the creature to maintain its normal lifestyle. Daytime temperatures and lighting are usually warmer and more intense than those at night.

You can, of course, make all adjustments manually. Following the sunrise-sunset chart in the newspaper for your region, you can turn your lights and tank/terrarium heaters on in the morning and off in the evening. Or you can let an electric timer do the on-off activation and can keep it accurate by changing the time weekly.

A reversed photocell will automatically do the job for you in its entirety.

No matter which method you use, the length of time your lighting is on each day should basically coincide with the hours of daylight in the region from where your turtle or tortoise originated.

POND TURTLES

*Of the four pond turtles found in the United States, only two—the wood turtle and the spotted turtle (*Glyptemys insculpta *and* Clemmys guttata, *respectively)— are now commonly kept pet species. The bog turtle,* Glyptemys muhlenbergi, *and the Pacific pond turtle,* Actinemys marmorata, *are protected and legally procured examples are now very expensive.*

Pond turtles require a varying degree of winter cooling to cycle reproductively. In the deep South, unless these turtles are artificially cooled, egg viability seems to drop off after two or three years. This seems especially true of wood turtles.

The Spotted Turtle

A small denizen of wooded ponds and bogs of eastern North America, the spotted turtle attains an adult length of only about 4 inches (10 cm). It seems most common in slightly acidic seeps and ponds that are heavily vegetated with sphagnum. In the early spring, while the weather is still chilly, the males may wander across country roadways in search of females.

The European pond turtle is a pretty and hardy basking turtle.

A few weeks later, egg-laden (gravid) females may wander in the same areas looking for suitable nesting sites. It is at these times that spotted turtles are most often encountered.

Appearance: Hatchlings, which are just over an inch (2.5 cm) in length when emerging from the egg, usually bear just a single yellow spot on each of the large dark gray carapacial scutes. Additional spots usually appear with advancing age and some old specimens are profusely speckled. Orange spots may occur on the neck and head, and the forelimbs and leg axils may vary in color from black to extensively orange.

Habits: Spotted turtles may estivate during the hottest part of the year and hibernate during the cold of winter. The spotted turtle is primarily an aquatic species and captives should be provided with a water area that is rather extensive, but not necessarily deep. The turtles should be able to access the land area easily

A young adult spotted turtle.

and at all points. They will thrive on the diet suggested for semiterrestrial turtle species (see page 45).

Wood Turtles

Once commonly seen over most of its range in the northeastern United States and immediately adjacent Canada, the wood turtle is now considered rare to imperiled. As with other creatures with which we share our world, the causes for population drops are severalfold. The most significant causes are habitat degradation (including fragmentation), extensive and often illegal collecting for the pet industry, and increased predation on nests and hatchlings.

Habits: The wood turtle, treated as a terrestrial turtle species by many hobbyists, is very much a semiaquatic. Although it often wanders and forages in woodlands and brushy meadows far from water, it swims readily, often breeds while in the water, and spends its lengthy period of dormancy in aquatic situations.

Appearance: The "woodie" is the larger species of the genus. Adults frequently exceed a shell length of 7.5 inches (19 cm). The carapacial color is of some shade of earthen brown, as are the top and sides of the head. The chin, neck, limbs, and tail vary (largely by geographic origin) from pale yellowish green (westerly populations) to brilliant red-orange (easterly populations).

The Bog Turtle

The bog turtle is a bog and streamside species in the North and a denizen of poorly drained, acidic mountain meadows, pastures, and woodland edges in the South. The bog turtle adult has

Wood turtles from the eastern states usually have brighter orange legs than those from the northcentral states.

a shell length of about 3.5 inches (9 cm), and is among the smallest of the world's turtle species.

Appearance: In coloration the carapace of the bog turtle is primarily brown to reddish brown. The scutes of the carapace may have poorly defined darker or lighter markings and/or lighter centers. The limbs may be extensively orange or mostly brown. Most specimens have a prominent patch of orange at the rear of the head. This may be in the form of a single large blotch or several smaller ones. Occasional specimens, especially old males, may have head blotches that are smaller, or lacking altogether.

Pacific Pond Turtles

The Pacific pond turtle is found in west-central Washington and western Oregon south to central Baja California.

Appearance: This is the least colorful of the Clemmys—olive-gray to olive-green with irregular and indistinctly defined lighter and/or darker marblings, reticulations, or radiations. The color of both the soft areas and the shell are quite similar, but the apexes of the limbs tend to be lighter hue.

TIP

Limited Availability

Neither the bog turtle nor the Pacific pond turtle are now common in the pet trade, despite the fact that both are bred in captivity.

Habits: Like the eastern spotted turtle, this is a highly aquatic form, seldom seen away from the water. The Pacific pond turtle is wary, takes fright easily, and dives quickly.

Two Exotic "Pond" Turtles

Turtles in various areas of the world parallel one another, not only in appearance, but in behavior and habitat preferences as well. Two that are quite similar to our pond turtles in their captive needs are the European pond turtle, *Emys orbicularis*, and the Asian pond turtle, *Chinemys reevesi*.

European Pond Turtle

Current studies indicate that rather than just one wide-ranging species, there are actually several species contained in this complex.

The European pond turtle, Emys orbicularis, is about to be broken into several full species.

Although the specimens in some populations do get larger, most European pond turtles are adult at between 4.5 and 6.5 inches (11.4–16.5 cm) in shell length. Besides ranging widely in Europe, these little turtles occur in northern Africa and western Asia.

Appearance: European pond turtles have a ground color of deep olive-brown, olive-black, or black. Carapacial markings are in the form of tiny dots, spots, or radiations of lighter (often yellow) pigment. The head and limbs, often as dark in color as the carapace, may or may not bear yellow(ish) spots.

Hatchlings are often more dully marked than the adults. Many hatchlings have profuse carapacial speckles of black or dark olive, rather than yellow. Yellow spots are visible on the sides of the head. These often take the form of two irregular stripes on each side.

Breeding: European pond turtles are now bred frequently in captivity. Not all females reproduce annually. Some, especially those from the more northerly portions of the range, produce eggs only biennially or even triennially. Winter cooling seems necessary, to successfully breed even the turtles from southern populations, and it has been suggested that an actual period of hibernation may be necessary to assure fertility in northern specimens.

Asian Pond (Reeve's) Turtle

Although it is often referred to as the "Japanese" Reeve's turtle, *Chinemys reevesi* actually has a distribution much greater than just Japan. It is also found over much of China and Korea.

Asiatic Reeve's turtles, **Chinemys reevesi,** *are of small size and are very hardy.*

Appearance: The carapace is tricarinate (triple-keeled), with the vertebral keel being the strongest and all keels being best defined on juvenile specimens. Concentric growth rings are retained throughout the turtle's life. Although specimens with shell lengths of more than 9 inches (22.8 cm) have been found, most are much smaller.

The carapace of this inveterate basker may vary from some shade of brown to nearly black. The scute seams are often noticeably darker. Males darken with advancing age. The head is dark with a yellow stripe on each side of the crown and variable reticulations on the cheeks and chin. The limbs are dark. The plastron is brown-blotched yellow.

Breeding: Females 5-inches (12.7 cm) long can produce viable eggs. Males are somewhat smaller than adult females and have a heavy, long tail. A weak plastral concavity is sometimes present. Captive breedings supply many hatchlings to the pet trade annually.

Females nest several times annually, depositing from 3 to 9 eggs each time. Newly hatched specimens are tiny—under an inch (2.5 cm) in length and much longer than wide. Like larger specimens, the babies are very hardy and, if given proper care, grow quickly.

Habits: The Asiatic pond turtle is a hardy, cold-tolerant species and personable, too. Some Asiatic pond turtles are overwintered in outdoor ponds in North Carolina and Virginia. They quickly accept captive conditions and readily associate the presence of a person with the introduction of food to their container. It is an omnivorous species, finding a wide variety of fruit, vegetables, and animal matter entirely are acceptable foods.

Aquatic turtles are all water-going turtles with basically flattened shells. However, a few of them are readily recognized as being different from the usual aquatic turtles.

Alligator Snappers and Common Snappers

The alligator snapping turtle, *Macroclemys temminckii*, and the common snapping turtle, *Chelydra serpentina*, are the only living members of the family Chelydridae. Both species are wholly aquatic. The alligator snapping turtle has no subspecies while the common snapping turtle has several.

The alligator snapper is found in larger river systems and lakes and oxbows of the southeastern coastal plain and the Mississippi River drainages. Adult males are among the world's largest freshwater turtles. Weights of more

*Cute and easily housed when hatchlings, adult common snapping turtles, **Chelydra s. serpentina**, become too large for most facilities.*

than 250 pounds (114 kg) and carapace lengths of more than 25 inches (63.5 cm) have been documented. The females are much smaller.

The common snapper (*Chelydra serpentina*) ranges southward from southern Canada, through the eastern two thirds of the United States, eastern Mexico and most of Central America to Ecuador. It is a denizen of ponds, lakes, flooded ditches, and slow rivers. The common snapper often reaches a carapace length of 12 inches (30 cm) and the record size is 19 inches (49.2 cm). A weight of 35 pounds (15 kg) is not uncommon; snappers weighing more than twice that have been found.

Appearance: The mud-brown coloration and roughened, serrate shells of the common and alligator snappers afford very effective camouflage in their watery lairs. Their strong jaws provide a formidable defense. Both genera have very small plastrons and very long tails. Dermal tubercles and projections are present

TIP

Handling Precautions

Be careful when handling snappers of either species. Babies can be lifted by merely enveloping them in your hand; larger specimens by grasping them securely by the rear of the shell. Even when this is done properly, the long neck of the common snapper will allow its mouth to nearly reach your fingers.

Larger specimens can be carefully (but securely) grasped by the tail and lifted. The plastron of the turtle must be nearest your leg so that the snapping mouth of the turtle is directed away from you. Very large specimens are best left alone or, if necessary, lifted with mechanical help. It is nearly impossible for one person to safely handle a viciously striking 60-pound (27 kg) turtle.

No matter how long they have been captives, many snappers of both species will continue to bite if restrained. They also will quickly come to associate the presence of food with that of their keeper and may snap upward in anticipation. Caution should always be foremost in your mind when associating in any manner with these big, powerful, and interesting chelonians.

on the sides of the head, chin, and neck. The neck of the alligator snapper is short and its head is massive. The neck of the common snapper is long and the head is proportionately smaller than that of its relative.

When viewed from above, the dorsolaterally directed eyes of the common snapper are easily visible; the laterally directed eyes of the alligator snapper are less easily seen. The alligator snapper has a worm-like appendage on its tongue. Both are most active at night.

Alligator snappers are not known to bask out of the water. However, common snappers sun not only on emergent snags and stumps, but on banks, sandbars, or leaning tree trunks. Frequently, common snappers thermoregulate by floating at the water's surface where their dark color quickly absorbs the sun's warming rays. Adults may also cross wide expanses of land when searching for a new territory.

Breeding

Because of their large size, neither of these turtles is commonly bred in captivity. Those that are bred are usually kept in large, outside pools rather than in indoor aquaria. Females lay one clutch annually and egg count can be from a half dozen (from small, young females) to more than four dozen (from females in their prime). Gravid females may nest only a few feet above the water line or may wander 150 or more feet (45.7 m) from the water before nesting. The smooth shelled eggs are roughly the size and shape of Ping-Pong balls. The incubation duration is from 65 to 125 days. Hatchlings measure about 1.5 inches (3.8 cm) in straight carapace length.

Hatchlings eat worms, fish, and tadpoles. Adults eat shellfish, crayfish, snails, other turtles, worms, insects, fish, amphibia, and even some aquatic plants.

The alligator snapper catches fish by opening its jaws widely and twitching the tongue animatedly. When not trying to catch a meal, the alligator snapper is not easily seen, even when its mouth is open. However, when the turtle is actively fishing, the double-ended appendage turns pink or red.

Hatchlings

Hatchlings of the alligator and the common snapping turtle are hardy and easily maintained as captives. Room temperature water, 76 to 82°F (24–27°C), is suitable. Slightly warmer (or temporarily slightly cooler) water will not harm these creatures. The water should be shallow enough to allow the turtle to breathe when its neck is mostly extended, because these turtles are poor swimmers. High water quality should always be maintained. Chlorine and chloramine additives should be removed whenever the water is changed. The ammonia content and pH of the water should be controlled by water changes or pertinent water additive.

A single small specimen will do well in a 10-gallon (40 L) tank. Should you be fortunate enough to live where the climate is benign enough to allow your turtle to live in a permanent shallow in-ground pool or other outside facility, so much the better.

Side-Necked Turtles

The term "side-neck" has been coined to describe the way that turtles in two families, the Pelomedusidae (primitive side-necks) and the Chelidae (advanced side-necks), withdraw their neck and head into the protection of their shell. The neck is folded in lateral rather than vertical curves and the head is tucked into the shoulder area.

The pelomedusine side-necks occur in northern South America, sub-Saharan Africa, Madagascar, and some of the Indian Ocean islands. The many species are primarily aquatic, but individuals of some may occasionally be found well away from water sources. This is especially true during the rainy season. One genus, *Pelusios*, the African mud turtle, apparently burrows into the earth to estivate/hibernate through the dry season.

Some species may emerge from the water to bask, especially when young. Others may simply crawl into shallow water or float at the surface of deeper water, exposing most or part of their carapaces to the sun. Many species get quite large; some are among the largest of freshwater turtles.

African Mud Turtles

Only Pelusios, the African mud turtles, have hinged plastra; all other genera have rigid plastra. Containing 14 species, *Pelusios* is also the largest genus in this family.

None among the many species of this genus is brightly colored, but all are immensely hardy creatures that seldom develop health problems in captivity. For this reason we strongly recommend small *Pelusios* sp. for beginning hobbyists. Of the many species contained in this genus, surprisingly few species are available to the pet trade. As a matter of fact, only two—the East African black mud turtle, *P. subniger*, and the West African mud turtle, *P. castaneus*—are regularly available to hobbyists. Although they are hardy, African mud turtles of all species often are aggressive toward other turtle species and occasionally toward human fingers.

Their jaws are strong, and aggression can quickly cause injury. The tails and trailing feet of basking turtles are often targeted by African mud turtles.

Both *P. subniger* and *P. castaneus* are rather smoothly domed turtles that may retain growth

Like many other turtles, the West African mud turtle is apt to kick sand over itself when ashore.

annuli well into adulthood. They have neither a vertebral keel nor posterior serrations. When submerged and inactive, these species may be likened in appearance to a stone with a head. Once they are acclimated, they are fairly active and are reasonably strong swimmers.

These turtles are bred by only a few hobbyists so many of the African mud turtles now offered in the pet trade are wild-collected imported specimens. In the wild, these turtles inhabit all manner of water holes, as well as swamps, marshes, and slowly flowing waters.

The East African mud turtle measures about 8 inches (20 cm) in length and the West African mud turtle is adult at about a foot (30 cm) in length. However, most examples seen in the pet trade are in the 3.5 to 5-inch (8.8–12.7 cm) size range. Sexually mature males have a slight plas-

tral concavity and a longer, thicker tail than the females.

African mud turtles of all species are primarily carnivorous and will eat a wide variety of natural and prepared foods.

Matamata

The advanced or chelid side-necks are separated from the primitive side-necks or pelomedusine side-necks by bone structure and the placement of the gular scute on the plastron. Chelids are found in South America, Australia, and New Guinea. These are also essentially aquatic turtles. Fewer than a half dozen species are generally available, but among those is the matamata, *Chelus fimbriatus*, the most spectacular in appearance of all turtles. The matamata is a typical chelid in that it folds its neck to the side to conceal its head. Curiously enough, it essentially is a nonswimmer, despite being wholly aquatic.

Appearance: The long, thick neck of the matamata is laterally flattened and fringed with filamentous appendages of skin. But it is the head of the matamata that usually generates the most interest. The head is broadly triangular, noticeably flattened, and the curved jaws form an apparent and perpetual smile. The nostrils extend forward in a doubly cylindrical snorkel. The eyes are small and easily overlooked. A pliable, flat flap of skin extends from each temporal area. The precise function of the cutaneous fringes and flaps that adorn the sides of the neck and chin remains largely conjectural. However, it is these flaps and fringes that yield the scientific name of *Chelus fimbriatus*, literally, the fringed turtle.

The fringes may help conceal the turtle by interrupting the outline. They may also serve as lures, when waving in the water, to bring fish prey closer. But the fringes of this turtle are highly innervated, and probably play a major role in prey detection and identification.

Habits: Despite their not inconsiderable size, when in habitat even adults of this normally slow-moving turtle can be easily overlooked. The rough shell of the matamata permits copious growths of algae to take hold, effectively concealing the turtle as a "wait-and-ambush" predator. While lying quietly, it waits for passing or inquisitive fish to come within the reach of the long neck. Then, with a forward lunge, and a corresponding distension of the throat, the widely opened maw sucks in water, fish, and all near it. The water and other unwanted debris are expelled, and the piscine prey swallowed. This method of hunting is often referred to as the "gape-and-suck" technique. In comparison with those of most turtles, the jaws of the matamata are weak. Its prey is swallowed whole in a series of gulping motions.

Occasionally matas may take a more active role in food procurement. We have seen ours actively pursuing fish, and even seeming to herd them into a corner of the tank where the fish are more vulnerable and easily caught.

The matamata is a denizen of the Amazon and Orinoco drainages in the South American countries of Bolivia, Peru, Ecuador, Colombia, and Brazil. It has also been found in Trinidad, but is thought to have been washed to that island by flood conditions.

Matas of all sizes are entirely aquatic. They must inhabit shallow water, or slow-moving or nonmoving water. All manner of backwaters, pools, oxbows, and lakes are favored. Despite its aquatic propensities, the matamata is, at best, a very short-term swimmer, drowning in water that other turtles negotiate with ease. Adult and young matas alike need water sufficiently shallow to allow them to rest on the bottom and merely extend their long necks upward to reach the surface.

Size: The record shell size for this remarkable turtle is just over 17 inches (43 cm). Most individuals are somewhat smaller. Females are slightly larger than the males. Males have a proportionately longer, heavier tail than the females.

Although no subspecies have been described, there appear to be a few rather constant geographical differences in both color and shell shape (when viewed from above) when the turtles of the Orinoco are compared with those of the Amazon.

These differences are especially noticeable in the juveniles. The juveniles of the Orinoco drainage have a tan-to-caramel-colored carapace, a dark marking on the central protuberance of each pleural scute, and a narrow, dark vertebral stripe. The dorsal surface of the broadly triangular head and thick neck are rather similarly colored, but have a dark-outlined, broad central area slightly darker in color. The throat and ventral surface of the neck are rose to strawberry. The axillae, ventral surfaces of the legs, and soles of the feet are paler rose. The plastron is light, often with pinkish overtones, and with a dark smudge at each lateral seam. When viewed from above, the sides of the carapace are nearly straight.

Although the Amazonian matas have the same markings, the ground color (especially those from Peru) is a much darker brown. When viewed from above, the carapace is broadly oval, having convex sides.

The current availability of matamatas in the pet trade is sporadic at best. The few that are imported command high prices.

Care: Matamatas are nonbasking species. They are easily kept in suitably sized aquariums that contain sufficient water for the turtles to move about easily, but that are sufficiently shallow so the matas do not need to swim to reach the surface to breathe.

In captivity many matamatas are quite active. Unless firmly anchored, all cage furniture will be persistently rearranged. Outside box filters should be used to help maintain water clarity and quality. Even with filtration it will be necessary to change most of the water weekly. A complete cleaning should be done monthly. Chlorines, chloramines, and other additives should be removed from the water.

Diet: It is simple to feed matas. Newly acquired specimens may insist on a live fish diet.

When sufficient prey items are available, matamatas grow rapidly. As captives, they quickly become accustomed to accepting dead fish and fish parts. Periodically place a capsule of multivitamin/mineral supplement in a proffered food item. It has been suggested that certain compounds present in goldfish are detrimental to the health of fish-eating reptiles. Therefore we use goldfish as dietary items only sporadically, providing minnows and shiners instead.

Breeding: Although the breeding biology of wild matamatas has often been reported, the species has proven rather difficult (but not impossible) to breed when captive. Up to 28 eggs have been reported from wild clutches.

To date, not only have captive clutches numbered considerably fewer, but hatching success has been relatively poor. Although wild matas reportedly prefer mud banks over sandbars for nesting, captives have accepted flat expanses of sand for nesting and deposition.

Captive incubation durations of the nearly spherical, hard-shelled eggs have averaged about 215 days. With a diameter of about 1.5 inches (3.5 cm), the eggs are slightly larger than Ping-Pong balls. Apparently, only a single clutch is produced annually.

Snake-Necks

The snake-necked turtles of southern South America, Australia, and New Guinea are also advanced side-necks. In all cases, the cervical vertebrae are longer than those of the trunk. In contrast to many of the short-necked members of this side-necked turtle family, the snake-necks are strong swimmers, and although common in quiet cochas, lagoons, oxbows, and billabongs, many species do not hesitate to enter deep and swiftly moving waters. South American snake-necks have proven very difficult to maintain in captivity.

Siebenrock's Snake-Necked Turtle
Chelodina siebenrockii

A New Guinea species, this turtle is currently the most readily available species. This narrow-shelled, olive-gray species attains a carapace length of about 12 inches (30 cm). It is a cold-sensitive turtle that must be kept warm year-round. All species are persistently aquatic, but some specimens wander a fair distance from water. Despite the fact that these turtles prefer to eat underwater, they are capable of eating on land.

Appearance: Except for *C. parkeri* of New Guinea, which has prominent light reticulations on its head, the Austro-Papuan snake-necks display no contrasting colors. The carapaces are olive-gray to black, the plastrons are usually light with dark pigment outlining each scute, limbs and dorsal surfaces of head and neck are pretty much the same color as the carapace, but the ventral surface of the neck and the chin are light (often yellowish). The comparative width of the forelobe of the plastron often figures prominently in species identification.

Snake-necks from temperate southern Australia do hibernate. Depending on the species, the carapace may be gently domed, somewhat flattened, or even have a weak to moderate longitudinal depression for the length of the carapace. The vertebral concavity may play an interesting role in reproduction in the populations that have it.

Males overtaking the females seem to orient themselves by following the concave vertebral area with their chin. However, specimens that lack the central concavity seem to do equally well in reproducing. Some males have noticeably concave plastrons while the plastrons of other are only weakly concave. Males have a much longer and thicker tail than the females. Although babies are easily kept in indoor aquaria, it is far easier to house the adults outside if possible. Adults thrive in 6-foot (1.8 m) diameter kiddie wading pools, sunk to their rim in the ground. The turtles are contained by a low fence a few feet from the pond.

Breeding: Although our seasons and photoperiods are reversed from those of Australia and New Guinea, snake-necks of most species will breed readily each summer. Females often nest as far from the "pond" as the confines of their enclosure would allow. The nests are about 5 inches (12.5 cm) deep and well able to accommodate the 5 to 12 eggs produced (some females are known to have produced up to two dozen eggs). With their long necks and rough shells, the babies are endearing creatures. They begin feeding as soon as the yolk sac is entirely absorbed and initially accept tiny (male guppy-sized) fish and chopped earthworms. The adults are fond of thawed frozen fish, worms, and trout and catfish chows. They will carefully comb through aquatic plants for snails and other organisms but do not seem to eat the plants themselves.

Red-Bellied Short-Necked Turtle
Emydura subglobosa

The red-bellied short-neck is the only member of this Australian and Papuan genus that is commonly seen in captivity. It attains an adult length of 9 inches (22.8 cm). It is an attractive side-necked turtle and the hatchlings are very contrastingly patterned.

Whether of normal color (top) or an albino, the red-bellied short-necked turtle, Emydura subglobosa, is an attractive pet species.

Although it fades to yellow as adulthood is approached, the plastron of hatchlings and juveniles is a very bright pink to pinkish-red. Yellow to reddish-pink stripes also occur on the head and neck. These fade in color as the turtle ages. The carapace is smoothly domed, nonserrate, and some shade of brown in color.

Breeding: Hatchlings offered for sale are usually captive bred and hatched. Many hobby-ists, both in the United States and Europe, work successfully with this attractive turtle. It seems that females attain sexual maturity at about 6.5 inches (16.5 cm) in carapace length. Males can be somewhat smaller. Courtship consists of head bobs and stroking of the female's head and neck by the male occur while the pair is swimming or hovering in the water.

Clutches contain from 3 (from small young females) to 12 (large adult females) eggs with from 5 to 7 being the norm. Several clutches may be produced in a season.

Females often nest in sunny, open areas several feet (1 m) from their pond, but some choose areas near the pond or against the base of a plant. The nests average 4 inches (10 cm) in depth and easily accommodate all eggs. The nests are not well hidden before the female departs.

Hatchlings of this species are alert and wary. On the occasions when they are approached while sunning, they scurry and tumble into the water.

A young adult albino Florida soft-shell, Apalone ferox.

Habits: Basking adults would allow us quite near them before tumbling into the water if we approached the enclosure slowly. Once in the water, they apparently felt more secure, and would take pieces of fish from our fingers. Besides fish, *E. subglobosa* readily accept trout and catfish chows, dried cat chow, snails, small mussels, crickets, and earthworms. They are a tropical species that must not be allowed to cool significantly in winter.

Soft-Shelled Turtles

Although they are every bit as recognizable as turtles as their hard-shelled relatives, the soft-shells, flattened and agile, are very different in many respects from typical turtles and are known affectionately as "animated flapjacks."

The soft-shelled turtles are classified in the family Trionychidae. They are of North American, African, Asiatic, and East Indian distribution. Although hatchlings and young of some Asiatic species are occasionally available in the pet trade, most are North American spiny soft-shells, smooth soft-shells, and Florida softshells.

The carapace length of the adults of some Asiatic soft-shells exceeds a yard (1 m)—in the case of the gigantic Asiatic, *Pelochelys bibroni*, more than 4 feet (1.2 m) in length. The largest North American species is the Florida soft-shell, adult females of which attain a carapace length

TIP

Water Acidification

Experiment with water acidification if you intend to maintain hatchling Florida softshells.

✔ Place six teabags placed for a few minutes in a small amount of boiling water
✔ Add that to 3 or 4 gallons (11.3–15.1 L) of aquarium water.

This is a starting point from which you can weaken or strengthen the solution.

Note the hemispherical protuberances on the anterior carapace of this male Florida soft-shell.

of just over 2 feet (.6 m); the largest recorded male is just half that size.

Habits: Although these strong swimmers are entirely at home in deep water, shallow river and lake edges are favored habitats. In these areas soft-shells will bury their shells into sand or mud and sit with only their necks and heads exposed. They like water sufficiently shallow so when the long neck is extended to the surface, they can breathe without uncovering themselves.

Appearance: The carapace of the soft-shelled turtles is covered with a tough leathery skin. The carapace, rounded or oval when viewed from above, may bear a series of points (spines) along the front edge. These spines are present on the American spiny soft-shells and the Florida soft-shell, but are absent on the smooth soft-shells. The forward edge of the carapace is flexible. The neck is very long and fully retractable, the head is elongate and in most cases terminates in a long, flexible snout. The feet are broad, the toes fully webbed, and a flange of skin extends along the top edge of each forelimb. The soft-shell turtle is ever ready to use its claws and jaws, especially when handheld.

Soft-shelled turtles are often the colors of the mud or sand bottoms where they are found. Babies of some species may have pretty and prominent carapacial spots. The carapacial spotting is usually retained into adulthood by the males but becomes obscure on the females.

TIP

Precautionary Note

While baby soft-shells are harmless, larger specimens can and will bite and scratch painfully. Handle them with care! All cage furniture for soft-shells—ornaments, substrate, basking platforms—must be nonabrasive.

A subadult eastern spiny soft-shell.

With the exception of hatchling Florida soft-shelled turtles, *Apalone ferox*, the members of this genus are easily maintained in captivity. Even the Florida species is easily kept once it has attained about 3.5 inches (9 cm) in length.

Skin problems: Speculation continues regarding the frequent skin problems of captive hatchling Florida soft-shelled turtles. Although they occur in the wild in both clear and murky ponds and lakes, in waters having a wide range of acidity and alkalinity (pH), and in both fresh and weakly brackish habitats, baby Florida soft-shells are extremely prone to bacterial and fungal skin disorders that are difficult to reverse and invariably lethal if not reversed. We have had identical episodes with captive-hatched babies and with babies taken from the wild.

Fungal problems may respond to a solution of acriflavine (follow directions of the package)

Like other soft-shells, eastern spiny soft-shells, **Apalone s. spinifer,** *are graceful and nimble swimmers.*

When ashore, soft-shelled turtles (such as this Chinese soft-shell, **Pelodiscus sinensis***) often kick sand all over themselves.*

or Betadyne in the water. Bacterial causes, of course, require a bactericide; since not all bacteria respond to the same medications, to effect a cure, veterinary diagnosis and intervention is often required. As often as not, both fungal and bacterial agents attack together, further complicating treatment.

The problem of skin lesions developing on captive aquatic snakes was at least partially addressed several decades ago by herpetologist/ showman, the late E. Ross Allen. While trying to maintain some of the difficult species, Allen began acidifying their aquarium water by adding freshly brewed tea in varying amounts. When combined with warmth—80 to 90°F (26.6–32.2°C)—skin lesions cleared. We have used this same concoction with hatchling

Florida soft-shelled turtles with what seems some benefit.

Substrate: Baby soft-shells may be maintained in a fully aquatic setup with a substrate of smooth, washed sand (sharp silica is apt to abrade the turtle's shell, giving fungal and bacterial problems an additional surface to invade). Soft-shells quickly bury themselves in the sand, often leaving only their head and snout exposed.

Unless a smooth platform (of Styrofoam, corkbark, or plastic) is wedged at the surface so the turtle can emerge if it chooses, the water should be shallow enough for the turtle to reach the surface for breathing without swimming. The water should be clean, filtered, and partially changed weekly (or more often if it becomes fouled).

The Gulf Coast smooth soft-shelled turtle, Apalone mutica calvata, *is the smallest of the North American soft-shells.*

Diet: Soft-shells eat all type of aquatic animal life in the wild and should be given worms (chopped if necessary), insects, and small fish (goldfish are not as good as shiners and minnows). Some prepared foods are acceptable to some soft-shells.

Appearance: When viewed from above, the Florida soft-shelled turtle is more oval than the smooth or the spiny soft-shells. The carapace of a baby is dark olive-green or olive-brown with darker oval ocelli. The carapace is rimmed with yellow posteriorly. This often shades to orange anteriorly. The dark head, neck, and limbs are spotted with yellow or orange. The plastron is gray anteriorly and charcoal posteriorly. This species has hemispherical projections on both the leading edge and anterior surface of the carapace.

Spiny and Smooth Soft-Shells

The Gulf Coast spiny soft-shell, *Apalone spinifera aspera*, and the midland smooth soft-shell, *A. m. mutica*, are also often seen in the pet trade. These two forms are much easier to maintain successfully in captivity than the Florida species.

Appearance: Both have carapaces of olive-tan. That of the smooth soft-shell is often more richly colored but has only indistinct dark markings. The dark underside of the carapace contrasts strongly in color with the light plastron. On the other hand, the underside of the rim of the carapace of the spiny soft-shelled turtle is nearly as light in color as the plastron. Spiny soft-shells (there are actually six rather similar subspecies) have many small dark spots and ocelli on the carapace and streaks that coalesce into either one or two dark lines on the top rear of the carapaces. Adult females of the smooth and spiny soft-shells are between 12 and 17 inches (30–43 cm) in length. Adult males may be only one-third the size of the females.

OTHER AQUATICS

Even the more typical aquatic turtles have their own quirks when it comes to defense, attracting a mate, appearance, and diet. Select the turtle that will be easiest for you to keep.

Mud and Musk Turtles

There are several genera of small to large, highly aquatic, very hardy but seldom-kept turtles classified in this family, the Kinosternidae. They are of New World distribution and may be encountered from New York and the Great Lakes states southward through the northern two thirds of South America.

Most have rugose and strongly keeled carapaces when small. While some retain the roughness and/or keeling throughout their lives, the shells of others smooth and dome with age. So thoroughly aquatic are these turtles that profuse, pattern-obscuring algal growths are not uncommon. Even at best, though, there is usually little pattern to obscure.

With age (adult, above) the red-cheeked mud turtle, **Kinosternon scorpiodes cruentatum,** *loses much of its juvenile brilliance.*

Genera

The two genera found in the United States, *Sternotherus*, the musk turtles, and *Kinosternon*, the mud turtles, are closely related. The entire assemblage has been gathered under the single generic name of *Kinosternon* by some authorities. The musk turtles are typified by reduced plastra with a single poorly developed hinge, while the plastrons of the mud turtles are proportionately larger and have a hinge at each end of the bridges (the bridges are the areas of shell on the sides which connect the carapace (upper shell) with the plastron (lower shell).

Appearance: Except for the facial coloring of the juveniles of the Latin American red-cheeked mud turtle, none of these turtles is brightly colored, even when a hatchling. The closest that any can come to brilliance is the salmon plastron of the hatchlings of the riverine loggerhead musk turtles, *Sternotherus minor* ssp., or the orangish plastron of the

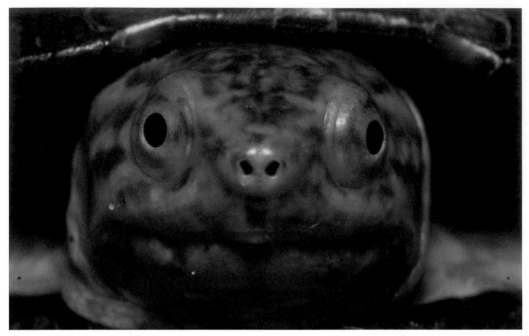

This is a juvenile white-chinned mud turtle, **Kinosternon scorpioides albogulare.**

quiet-water common mud turtles, *Kinosternon subrubrum* ssp. The plastral colors quickly fade as these turtles of the eastern United States attain their 4.5 inch (11.4 cm) adult size.

Hatchlings of the Central American red-cheeked mud turtle, *K. scorpioides cruentatum*, have variable amounts of red or orange on the sides of the head, and some are startlingly beautiful. The red usually begins to fade during the second or third year of the turtle's life. Some adult red-cheeked mud turtles remain quite pretty while others lose almost all traces of red. This turtle is adult at from 4 to 7 inches (10–17.5 cm) in length.

Several of the musk and mud turtles may have prominent yellow stripes on their faces when young (common musk turtle, *Sternotherus odor-*

atus, and striped mud turtle, *K. bauri* among them) but these stripes usually fade and often fragment as the turtles age. Besides facial stripes, the striped mud turtle also has three well-defined to obscurely defined yellow(ish) carapacial stripes. These are usually brightest on juvenile specimens.

The closest a mud turtle comes to a light shell color is seen on the olive-yellow to olive-green 5-inch (12.7 cm), yellow mud turtle, *Kinosternon flavescens* ssp., of the central United States. The throat of this last species is much more yellow than its shell.

Mexican Giant Musk Turtles

The largest members of this family are from southern Mexico and northern Central America. These are the always-ready-to-bite Mexican

This striped-necked musk turtle, **Sternotherus minor peltifer,** *makes a very hardy and long-lived captive.*

giant musk turtles (genus *Staurotypus*), which attain an overall carapace length of about 13 inches (33 cm). These turtles are placed in the family Staurotypidae by some researchers. Babies are occasionally available in the pet trade, and are pleasingly colored in a dark speckled variable gray.

Although Mexican giant mud turtles dull in color as they age, the strongly tricarinate (three keels) carapace of babyhood is retained and may even accentuate as the turtle grows. Of all of the musk and mud turtles, this big, highly adaptable species may be the only one captive bred in any significant numbers. This is not because they are difficult to breed, but rather, because they are not sought by most advanced hobbyists.

Habits: The rather sedentary lifestyles of the musk and mud turtles make them very amenable to captive conditions. Although often referred to as "nonbaskers," most species actually do seek the sun in one manner or another. Some bask by lying quietly in sun-warmed shallow water with all or part of their carapace exposed. Others may actually climb clear of the water on mudbars or protruding snags or other debris, or actually climb rather high into waterside trees. From such basking platforms startled musk or mud turtles may occasionally drop into boats passing beneath.

Although they are initially shy, musk and mud turtles soon come to recognize that the presence of a person often means that food

Mud turtles have a hinge fore and aft of the bridge (the part of the shell that connects the carapace to the plastron).

becomes available. These turtles have strong jaws and can be aggressive toward basking turtles if the latter are housed with them. The jaws of the kinosternids are strong and the injuries caused can be grave.

Although they will do well in spartan quarters, the musk and mud turtles certainly deserve better. These turtles will thrive if kept in well-filtered aquariums with rock caves, growing aquatic plants, and an easily accessed, warmed, illuminated, and exposed basking platform. Curved corkbark pieces firmly wedged between the sides of the aquarium will make an easily accessed, safe haulout.

Diet: Musk and mud turtles are primarily carnivorous. They eagerly accept worms, aquatic insects, crickets, pieces of raw meat and fish, as well as prepared trout, catfish, and cat chows.

Remember also the propensity of these turtles for climbing. You must be certain that they cannot escape by clambering up a filter stem or air hose, or by reaching the top rim of the tank from their basking platform.

Map Turtles

The map turtles of the genus *Graptemys* are remarkable for their extreme sensitivity to unclean water conditions and for the size differentiation between the males and the females. Adult females of the larger species can attain a 10-inch (25 cm) carapace length. The once-

The Texas map turtle, Graptemys versa, *is a rather small and very attractive species.*

bright females also tend to fade in color and pattern as they age. Males, on the other hand, are adult at about 4.5 inches (11 cm) in length—some may attain 6 inches (15 cm)—and retain the brilliance of the hatchlings.

Riverine Gems

The dozen species are found in river systems and nearby ponds and lakes of the central and eastern United States. The greatest concentration of species, several of them of endangered status, occurs in the river systems of Alabama, Florida, Louisiana, and Mississippi.

Narrow-headed and Broad-headed

The map turtles are informally divided by appearance into the "narrow-headed" and the "broad-headed" species. Some of the smaller narrow-headed species (several of which are endangered) are reasonably hardy throughout

their lives if kept in clean, filtered water. The adult males, as well as hatchlings and juveniles of both sexes of even the big, broad-headed species, may be maintained with relative ease.

━━━━ TIP ━━━━

Skin Fungus

It is almost impossible to do anything wrong with adult map turtles; however, if water quality is unsatisfactory, babies will develop skin fungus. This is easily eradicated with methylene blue or Acriflavine (remedies sold in tropical fish stores), but it is better not to have the problem, by making certain the water in which the baby turtles live is always clean.

The red-ear mark so typical of the subspecies becomes obscured on melanistic red-eared sliders.

The importance of clean, filtered water to the health of the map turtles cannot be overemphasized. Without nearly absolute cleanliness, map turtles are very prone to disfiguring and potentially fatal shell lesions.

Appearance: The map turtles derive both common and generic names from the intricate carapacial markings. These light lines, forming circles, blotches, and reticulations, are best defined on the hatchlings and juveniles. However, of the species in which the females attain great size, the smaller adult males also are often prominently marked.

Babies of several forms of map turtles are frequently offered in the pet trade. Several additional species, including endangered forms, are rather regularly offered by specialty reptile dealers. (See comments on the laws governing the sale of endangered turtles, page 39).

Diets: Map turtles are highly carnivorous. The diet of the several narrow-headed forms and the juveniles and males of the broad-headed forms consists largely of aquatic insects, small crayfish, snails, and other such water-dwelling fare. The diet of the females of the various broad-headed map turtles changes as these turtles mature.

Adult female common, false, Alabama, Barbour's, Escambia, and Pascagoula map turtles develop conspicuously enlarged heads, strengthened jaw muscles, and flattened crushing (alveolar) plates behind the mandibles. Adult females of these six map turtle species feed largely on crayfish, gastropods, and bivalves. Needless to say, a bite by an adult female of any of these forms would be unpleasant. In captivity most examples will accept high-quality prepared turtle foods.

Habits: Map turtles, as a group, are highly aquatic and extremely wary. Preferentially, map turtles bask regularly on protruding snags, brush, and sandbars that are either water-surrounded or spacious, peninsula-like expanses.

The taxonomy of many of the map turtles is controversial. This is especially true in the Ouachita/false/Mississippi map turtle group. Scientific designations may vary in other listings.

When attempting to identify these mentioned map turtles, one must consider the following:

1. What is the arrangement of the spots on the head?

2. Is there a vertical crescent?

3. Are these spots behind the eye?

4. What is the shape of the spots?

5. Are the spots vertically or horizontally oriented?

6. Are spots present on the mandibles?

To make a difficult task even more difficult, where ranges of subspecies (species?) of map turtles overlap, intergradation (hybridization?) occurs. To even attempt identification of some of these specimens, it is necessary to have an up-to-date field guide in hand, and to extrapolate as well.

The Mississippi map turtle, G. pseudogeographica kohni, is the most commonly offered of the baby map turtles. In this species the plastron is more prominently and intricately patterned than the carapace. Mississippi map turtles are best identified by the presence of a big yellow (sometimes fragmented) crescent behind each eye. Even if incomplete, no other head stripes extend past it to the eye.

The false map turtle, G. p. pseudogeographica, is also frequently seen in the pet trade. Rather than a crescent, the false map turtle has an often transverse elongate spot or two behind each eye, but some of the lower head stripes reach the eye. There are no prominent light spots on the mandibles of either of these map turtles.

The Ouachita map turtle, G. o. ouachitensis, has a roughly rectangular longitudinal blotch behind the eye, a light spot beneath each eye, and a light spot, posteriorly on each side of the lower jaw. The very closely allied Sabine map turtle, G. ouachitensis sabinensis, by others, is nearly identical, but the postocular blotch is oval rather than rectangular. These map turtles all have a low but well-defined vertebral keel.

The common map turtle, which occurs over much of the same range as the previous four, has an irregular blotch behind the eye, a widened yellow line behind the mouth, and only a weakly keeled carapace.

Sawbacks

Sawbacks are small map turtles that occur in the major river systems of Mississippi, adjacent Louisiana, and Alabama.

Appearance: The center rear of the first three vertebral scutes projects strongly upward, producing a serrate appearance when viewed from the side. Of the three, the ringed, G. oculifera, and the yellow-blotched, G. flavimaculata, are listed as endangered species. A very few captive-bred and hatched babies are occasionally available at prices that reflect this scarcity.

The black–knobbed sawback, G. nigrinoda ssp., (represented by two races) is not considered endangered. It is rather regularly seen in the pet trade. This small and beautiful turtle is restricted in distribution to three river systems in southern Alabama.

Hatchling western painted turtles are barely the size of a quarter.

Females of all of these saw-backed species attain a shell length of about 7.5 inches (19 cm). Males are only half that size.

Cagle's map turtle, *G. caglei*, of southeastern Texas is one of the prettiest of the map turtles. It is currently a candidate for listing as a federally endangered species. It is another of the narrow-headed insect eaters and is brilliantly and intricately marked. It is captive-bred in very small numbers. Cagle's map turtle is similar in size to the black-knobbed sawback.

Painted Turtles

The painted turtles, *Chrysemys*, are pet-store favoritese. They are rather closely related basking turtles that arc now found across the United States from coast to coast and border to border.

Diets: They are largely carnivorous when young, but many are essentially herbivorous when adult. Babies eat snails, tiny leeches and worms, aquatic insects, tadpoles, dying or dead fish, and other carrion. Some plant material is also eaten. The adults of many species reverse these dietary preferences, first seeking plant material and secondarily ingesting animal matter. Captives thrive on a combination of prepared foods (various turtle diets, trout chow, catfish chow, and dog chow) and leafy greens. Aquatic vegetation (*Valisneria, Sagittaria, Elodea, Hydrilla*, and the like) is especially favored by these turtles.

Habits: These turtles become active each spring soon after most of the ice has melted from their ponds, and remain active until the ice has virtually mantled their ponds again the following winter. Painted turtles are hardy

Of the four races of painted turtle, only the southern painted, Chrysemys picta dorsalis, *has an orange vertebral stripe.*

Southern painted turtles may often be seen basking at the edges of shallow water habitats.

beasts, and they will thrive as captives if provided with clean water, suitable basking areas, and nutritious foods. They can withstand warmth, cold, and all the ranges between.

Northern painted turtles can winter outside in all of the northern United States and southern Canada, if hibernating provisions are made, and if their pond does not freeze all of the way to the bottom.

Both northern and southern specimens can be wintered outside in our southern tier states with little or no preparation. The important thing to remember is that they be allowed to thermoregulate and to feed when so inclined.

Of the four subspecies of painted turtles, it is the southern, *C. picta dorsalis,* of the Mississippi drainage south of Illinois and the western, *C. p. bellii,* of northern Oklahoma and Illinois west to

Oregon and British Columbia and California that are most often offered in the pet trade.

Appearance: The southern painted turtle, identified by a prominent orange vertebral stripe, is the smallest—to 5.5 inches (14 cm)— of the four races. The western painted turtle, which occasionally exceeds 9 inches (22.8 cm) in carapace length (but is usually smaller), is the largest race. It has a netlike reticulum of light (sometimes red) lines on the carapace and a red plastron that bears a light-centered dark central blotch with arms that follow the scute seams, sometimes to the edge of the plastron.

The two remaining races, the eastern (6 inches [15.2 cm]), and the midland (5.75 inches [14.6 cm]), are between the other races in size. It can be hard to differentiate between the eastern

*At an adult length of 10 inches (25 cm),
the western painted turtle,* Chrysemys
picta belli, *is the largest subspecies.*

and midland painted turtles. This is especially so
in areas where intergradation is common.

Range: The range of the eastern painted turtle, *C. p. picta*, pretty much follows the eastern
seaboard from Nova Scotia to central North Carolina, where it then follows the Piedmont and
mountain provinces inland to central Georgia.

The midland painted turtle, *C. p. marginata*,
is found essentially west of the eastern turtle's
range, from Canada southward to Tennessee,
and dipping down to Alabama and northeastern
Georgia. The eastern painted turtle has an
unmarked or unpatterned, solid-colored plastron and the carapacial scutes are bordered
with olive and arranged pretty much in straight
rows. The midland painted turtle has a solid
lengthwise dark blotch on the plastron (no

outward extending arms) and the vertebrals are
not in line crossways with the costal scutes.

Breeding: A female painted turtle (especially
the most northerly ones) may not lay eggs every
year. On years that she does lay, she may produce
several clutches of from 4 to 10 (rarely to 18)
eggs. The interval between nestings is from two
to three weeks (longer if weather is unseason-
ably cool and metabolism is slowed). The nests
are several inches (about 8 cm) deep, easily
accommodating all of the eggs with ample room
left for a thick earthen cover. The nests are dug
in open, sunlit areas. Somewhat less than three
months is required for incubation. Late hatchlings have been known to overwinter in the nest.

Painted turtles are excellent pets, especially
in garden pools. If kept in clean, quasi-natural
conditions, their lifespan may exceed 15 years.
The known record for a captive is slightly more
than 20 years.

Sliders

What does "slider" mean? It refers to the tendency these turtles have when they are startled:
they slide into the water.

The two best known sliders are the red-eared
slider, *Trachemys scripta elegans*, and the yellow-
bellied slider, *T. s. scripta*. Once restricted to the
southeastern United States, the red-eared slider
is now found over much of the world, due to
prolific released pets. A third race, the Cumberland slider, *T. s. troosti*, occurs in Tennessee's
Cumberland Plateau region. Several Latin American forms are known.

Appearance: Red-eared sliders regularly attain
a shell length of 9 inches (22.8 cm). More rarely
they may near 11 inches (27.9 cm) in length. The
plastron of the red-eared slider bears prominent

The Big Bend slider, Trachemys gaigeae, *is one of the prettiest turtles of the United States.*

ocelli, and the common name is derived from the broad red stripe behind each eye. That same reddish stripe is shared by virtually all of the tropical forms, but not by the other two United States races. In fact, rather than a stripe, the yellow-bellied slider has a bright yellow blotch behind each of its eyes. This conspicuous marking is brightest in juveniles and female specimens, but is an excellent field mark when present.

The plastron of the hatchling yellow-bellied sliders bears ocelli anteriorly but is usually immaculate posteriorly. The plastral markings fade with advancing age and are often present on older examples as poorly defined dusky smudges.

Brazilian sliders are beautiful when young, but darken with age.

This pretty adult red-ear is from the south-Texas population.

The green shell color of all subspecies fades with age. It is retained most strongly by female specimens. Males' shells darken with age and may appear to be mostly or entirely black. One or more strains of albino redeared sliders have been developed and are now commonly available. Even more recently, interestingly colored forms called "pastels" have become available. Although some pastels may be the result of temperature manipulation during incubation, others seem genetically determined. Temperature-manipulated pastels may often be determined by their fragmented shell scutes and curiously truncated snouts.

Cooters

Cooter is derived from "kuta," a word of African origin that means turtle.

River cooters are most commonly encountered in waters that are moving, no matter how slowly. The coastal plains and red-bellied cooters often inhabit flooded, heavily vegetated ditches, ponds, and lakes.

The three species most commonly seen in the pet trade are the common river cooter, *Pseudemys c. concinna*, and Peninsula cooter, *P. floridana peninsularis*, and the Florida red-bellied cooter, *P. nelsoni*.

All of these cooters grow to more than 15 inches (38.1 cm) in length.

Appearance: As hatchlings, both the hieroglyphic river cooter and the Peninsula cooter are little green turtles with variable yellow markings on head, neck, limbs, and carapace. The former, a resident of the rivers systems of the Gulf and southeastern Atlantic drainages, tend to have the carapacial markings in the form of rings (circles). The plastron is reddish with dark markings following the scute seams.

With growth, the color of this turtle fades to grayish and the rings of babyhood fade.

Suwannee cooters, **Pseudemys concinna suwanniensis,** *are one of the largest of the basking turtles in the United States.*

Instead, the carapace of the adult is marked with light dots, dashes, circles, spirals, and bars—hieroglyphics, if you will. The most consistent of these markings is a well-defined letter "C" on the second carapacial scute. The plastron retains the dark seam markings but fades to pale yellow.

The most definitive markings of the Peninsula cooter, at any age, are a pair of light yellow hairpins on the neck, the closed end behind each eye. The carapace of the adult is dark. Light vertical markings may be prominent or obscure. The plastron of both hatchlings and adults is an unmarked yellow.

Florida Red-bellied Turtle

One of the prettiest of cooters offered in the pet trade is the Florida red-bellied turtle. This is another large species, often attaining a carapace length of 12 inches (30 cm) and rarely more than 14 inches (35 cm).

Appearance: The babies are green, with head stripes that are less numerous than those of their congeners. The shaft of a yellow arrowlike marking lies between the eyes, with the point on the snout. The plastron of the babies is usually some shade of orange (rarely more yellow than orange). Adults darken but often develop

The Florida red-bellied cooter, Pseudemys nelsoni, *is beautiful both as an adult (top) and as a hatchling.*

a broad vertical orange or red bar on each costal scute.

The plastron may fade to yellow centrally but usually retains orange edges. Intergrading (interbreeding of subspecies) and hybridizing (interbreeding of species) can make identification of these big basking turtles even more confusing than normal. Consider all characteristics on problematic specimens.

Diet: Sliders, cooters and painted turtles forage and swallow while in the water, utilizing both sight and smell to find foodstuffs. If kept indoors, babies of these species can live in filtered aquariums that are prettily planted and landscaped. With growth, the turtles begin to consider their plantings as food.

Habitat: Because of their large size, adults are best kept as garden pool turtles. Those from the more temperate areas of the United States are quite cold-tolerant; tropical races and those from the Florida peninsula and lower Rio Grande valley are less so. Warmth-adapted species should be brought into an indoors aquarium during periods of cold weather. If protected from freezing and offered hibernation facilities, the more northerly forms can be kept out year-round in most areas.

Since basking is both psychologically and physiologically important to turtles in these genera, it is important that the garden pool be located in a sunlit area. Soft sunny banks and snags projecting over and from the water should be provided.

Breeding: Mating occurs in the water. Courtship varies by species and subspecies. The males of some forms have elongated claws and hover in the water in front of the female,

River cooters, Pseudemys c. concinna, *are beautifully colored and precisely patterned.*

caressing her face and anterior shell with trembling claws. The males of short-clawed forms pursue the female, nipping at the trailing edge of her shell. In both cases, when the female becomes quiescent, copulation occurs.

Nesting in well-drained areas, the female sliders, cooters, and painted turtles may produce multiple clutches, depositing from as few as 2 to more than 20 eggs. Depending on temperature and nest humidity, incubation can vary from about two months to nearly three months. Incubation temperatures should be maintained between 82 and 87°F (28–30°C) (see comments on incubation temperatures, page 30).

LAND-GOING TURTLES AND TORTOISES

The land-going tortoises and box turtles need water only to drink, which makes it easier to keep their enclosures clean than the aquatic species. However, these chelonians have distinct caging and dietary needs.

Box Turtles

Box turtles are probably the most readily recognized turtles of America. Despite being land dwellers like the tortoises, these highly domed denizens of woodland (eastern subspecies) and brushy prairies (western subspecies) are more closely allied to the painted and spotted turtles than to the tortoises.

Photographs often show box turtles posed among wild strawberries or blackberries, but box turtles actually prefer snails, slugs, worms, and insects for food. Not only do they prefer hard-to-find dietary items, but they can be difficult to acclimate to captive conditions. This seems especially so when "crossover of habitat" occur.

Hobbyists in the western United States often find the eastern box turtles, *Terrapene carolina*

This immense male African spurred tortoise, Geochelone sulcata, is nearing 200 pounds (90 kg) in weight.

ssp., more consistently difficult to acclimate in that area of the country than the native, more arid-adapted western (or ornate) box turtles, *T. ornata* ssp. Similarly, eastern hobbyists find the western box turtles difficult to acclimate. Thus it seems that captives of the two species (there are many subspecies) do best in their respective homelands—where they are preadapted to the vagaries in humidity, temperature, and food items.

The plastron: Box turtles derive their common name from the ability of the adults to draw the plastron upward against the bottom of the carapace to protect the withdrawn head, limbs, and tail. The cartilaginous hinge is located in the suture between the pectoral and abdominal scales of the plastron. The hinge is undeveloped at hatching, but becomes fully developed by the time the turtle is about one quarter grown. However, during times of plenty, when worms and grasshoppers are abundant and the berry season is in full swing, box turtles may become so corpulent that they are unable to entirely close their plastron.

Sexing: To accurately sex box turtles, check the secondary sexual characteristics. Certain of these characteristics may vary subspecifically.

✔ The tail of adult male box turtles is thicker and somewhat longer than that of the female. This holds true for all subspecies.

✔ Adult males of all but the three-toed box turtle have a plastral concavity in the rear lobe of the plastron. This concavity may or may not be present on male three-toed box turtles. It often isn't.

✔ Adults males of the eastern and Gulf Coast box turtles often have red irides (irises); those of the females are yellow or brown. This is not invariable. Rarely females have red eyes, but the irides are usually not the bright red of the eyes of the males. The irides of male three-toed box turtles may be reddish, but often aren't.

✔ Males of all subspecies tend to have curved, hooklike claws on their hind feet. The claws of the females are straighter.

Photoperiod: All races of the eastern box turtle are protected by law in most of the states in which they occur, but despite this protection eastern box turtles seem less common over much of their range today than in past decades. Loss of suitable habitat, including habitat fragmentation, vehicular deaths as the creatures cross highways, collecting for the pet trade, and increased predation by a burgeoning number of predators (ants, raccoons, opossums, armadillos, foxes, and domestic dogs among them) on an ever-decreasing number of box turtle nests have all contributed to the population decline of the eastern box turtles.

Eastern Box Turtles

Eastern box turtles are divided into subspecies that usually have three toes, but sometimes have four toes on the hind feet (three-toed, Mexican, and Florida) and those that usually have four, but sometimes have three toes on the hind feet (Gulf-Coast, Yucatan, and eastern).

Subspecies: Of the six recognized subspecies of the eastern box turtle, four occur in the eastern United States and two in Mexico. Only the four races of the United States are seen in private collections.

The nominate eastern form occupies the largest range. It is known scientifically as *T. c. carolina* and because many specimens are prettily colored in yellow, oranges, and warm browns

The Florida box turtle, **Terrapene carolina bauri,** *is a pretty terrestrial turtle that seems to be declining in numbers.*

The eastern box turtle, **Terrapene c. carolina**, *still a popular pet, is now protected over much of its range.*

(others may be quite drab), it is the subspecies usually depicted on posters and magazine covers. This highly domed, oval turtle is found from northern Florida to Massachusetts and from Michigan to northwestern Mississippi. It is a meadow-edge and open-woodland species. It usually has four toes on the hind feet. Although it is often found near pond and lake edges as well as along woodland and damp meadow streams, the eastern box turtle seldom enters water more than 1 or 2 inches (2.5–5 cm) in depth. If it is forced into or accidentally topples into deep water, it usually bobs on the surface like a cork while paddling clumsily toward the nearest shore.

The southeasternmost representative of the clan is the Florida box turtle, *T. c. bauri*. It is entirely unlike its more northerly cousin in both appearance and color. The black (or nearly black) carapace is elongate and marked with well-delineated radiations of yellow. The rear of the carapace flares outward. The proportionately narrow carapace is very highly domed. There are two yellow lines (these are sometimes fragmented) on each side of the head.

This race, which for all intents and purposes is endemic to Florida, is fully protected. You can be reasonably sure that specimens now offered in

the pet trade have been gathered in violation of conservation laws.

Populations of the Florida box turtle have also been adversely impacted by habitat reduction and fragmentation. The draining of even temporary wetlands adversely affects populations. Damp open woodlands, damp meadows, marshes, and swamp edges are favored habitats of this box turtle. They seldom enter deep water voluntarily.

The Gulf Coast box turtle, *T. c. major*, often enters water and may be seen walking along the bottom of rather deep canals and waterholes of various kinds. It is the largest of the eastern box turtle subspecies, and although highly domed, has the carapace rather flattened centrally, and the marginals widely flared along the posterior edges.

This is a dull-colored turtle that is as likely as not to be devoid of strongly contrasting carapacial colors. Old males often have a chalk-white moustache or moustache and sideburns facial markings. In its pure, nonintergraded form, the Gulf Coast box turtle occurs only on Florida's panhandle. However, intergrade specimens showing much Gulf Coast box turtle influence may be

The Gulf Coast box turtle, Terrapene carolina major, *is the largest and most aquatic of the predominantly terrestrial eastern box turtles. This is a subadult specimen.*

encountered from eastern Louisiana to central Georgia. This big box turtle is at home in the moist woodlands and marsh edges of its rather small range. It is protected over most of its range.

The three-toed box turtle, *T. c. triunguis,* is the most divergent subspecies. It ranges widely from Missouri and Alabama to eastern Texas and Kansas. Although some specimens may be rather brightly colored, many show a tendency toward a unicolored olive-brown, olive-tan, or horn-colored carapace. Adult males may have a fair amount of red or maroon on the head. Most males lack the plastral concavity so predominant in males of other subspecies.

Courtship: The courtship of the eastern box turtle is similar to that of many other turtles and tortoises. The male circles and butts females he encounters, nipping at the front of their shell, limbs, and head. If the female is receptive she allows copulation.

A month to six weeks later, the female digs a nest in a root-free area in relatively soft, well-drained soil that receives sunlight for at least part of the day. From two to eight (often four or five) eggs are laid. Multiple clutches are normal. In the northern portion of the range, hatchling box turtles have been known to overwinter in the nest.

Habits: In the North, box turtles hibernate (brumate) for several of the coldest months. There are times when they seem to make surprisingly little effort to seclude themselves. In western Massachusetts, box turtles have been found hibernating with the top of their carapace virtually at ground level. Although the snow does have an insulating quality, the fact that the ground was frozen beneath the turtle and the fact that the turtle emerged from its hibernaculum unscathed indicate other physiological changes occur for protection from the subfreezing temperatures. See pages 25–29, for guidelines on how to hibernate box turtles kept in captivity.

All of the eastern box turtles require a high to moderate relative humidity, with the prairie populations of the three-toed species requiring least.

Western Box Turtles

Much of what we have said for the eastern box turtles applies to the two races of the western box turtle as well. Since the eastern box turtle is largely protected, these two box turtles, the vividly marked ornate, *T. o. ornata* and, more rarely, the pallid desert *T. o. luteola*, have become the types most frequently seen in the pet trade of the United States and Europe. They are pretty but seem even more difficult to acclimate and establish in captivity than their eastern relatives.

Western or Eastern?

Differentiating between the western and eastern box turtles isn't difficult. At first, the ornate box turtle may be mistaken for a Florida. However, the dark carapace of the ornate box turtle is not so highly domed; in fact it is flattened centrally. Additionally, the prominent radiating yellow lines of its carapace seem heavier and not quite as precisely delineated as the carapacial markings of the Florida box turtle. Rather than bearing two prominent light lines on each side of the head like the Florida box turtle, the head of the ornate box turtle is usually prominently spotted.

The dark plastron of the ornate box turtle is heavily patterned with bold light lines; the plastron of the Florida box turtle is light, occasionally with a few dark markings. If present, these markings are best defined along the scute sutures and on the anterior lobe of the plastron.

Desert or Ornate?

The ground color of the desert box turtle is considerably lighter than that of the ornate. Additionally, the light carapacial markings of the desert subspecies are thinner and more numerous, but usually do not contrast sharply with the ground color. All markings are best defined on young specimens; old specimens may be an almost unicolored yellowish tan or horn-color.

Range: As mentioned earlier, the two races of the western box turtle are creatures of open plains, prairies, and related scrub and low brush thickets. Although the desert race inhabits the driest habitats, it often chooses irrigated areas and the environs of water-holes and river edges for its microhabitat. *Terrapene o. ornata* occurs in patches of suitable habitat from Indiana and South Dakata to the lower Rio Grande Valley. *Terrapene o. luteola* ranges over much of far

The ornate box turtle, **Terrapene o. ornata,** *is beautiful but can be difficult to acclimate—especially in humid climates.*

The orange facial flush of the Chinese yellow-rimmed box turtle is more intense during the breeding season.

western Texas, westward to New Mexico and southward across the Rio Grande into adjacent Mexico.

Breeding: Unlike the reproductive strategies of the eastern box turtles, which involve much "courtship," the breeding sequence of the western box turtle is often more straightforward. When a male western box turtle encounters a receptive female (pheromone production quite probably plays a considerable role in determining receptivity) he often merely scurries forward and mounts her. Some males will stop to sniff the rear margin of the female's shell, to redetermine receptivity. Some males will sniff and butt the female, but many, especially captives, dispense with all courtship formalities. The male ornate box turtle has the innermost toe enlarged and angled differently from the others. This helps him in positioning during breeding. The nesting

sequence and clutch size is similar to that of the eastern box turtle.

Except in the lower Rio Grande valley, where the ornate box turtle is active for all but a few days of the year, both races of the western box turtle hibernate for the several months of winter.

Asian Box Turtles

Many of the Asian box turtles were once popular with hobbyists. However, only two species remain commonly seen. These two are the aquatic Malayan box turtle, *Cuora amboinensis*, and the terrestrial yellow-margined box turtle, *Cuora flavomarginata*. Since these have plastral hinges and can close every bit as tightly as the American box turtles, we will discuss them here.

The Malayan box turtle actually ranges well beyond the confines of Malaya. Besides Malaya, it occurs from the Philippines to the Nicobars and from Vietnam through Thailand. It is one of the most aquatic and least colorful of the genus. The smoothly rounded carapace of an adult varies, by population, from somewhat flattened to highly domed, and is black in color. The plastron is yellowish, as are the soft body parts; the limbs are dark. The dark head and neck are prominently striped with yellow. The uppermost pair of stripes (one on each side) converge on the tip of the snout. The hatchlings are dark and have three dorsal keels (tricarinate). This is a rather slow-moving, shy turtle. Imports are quick to withdraw into the safety of their shell and may remain immobile and withdrawn for long periods. Although most are considerably smaller, the Malayan box turtle does occasionally attain a shell length of 8 inches (20 cm).

Habits: Captives of this quiet, inoffensive turtle seem quite omnivorous. They eat all manner of nonnoxious water plants, romaine, escarole, and other dark leafy vegetables, a fair variety of fruit, snails, worms, crayfish, and prepared foods such as trout, catfish, and dog chows. Although it has been elsewhere stated that the species is preferentially herbivorous, even our fresh imports have accepted animal matter as readily as plants.

Breeding: If sexually mature and cycled through a natural photoperiod, females of the Malayan box turtle may deposit several sets of two eggs at about two-week intervals. This species can be tough to sex. Some males have a plastral concavity. About the only invariable is the proportionately longer and heavier tail of sexually mature males.

The yellow-margined box turtle is the most popular of the Asian box turtles with hobbyists. Its scientific name is *Cuora flavomarginata*. Most specimens available in the pet trade are wild-

Hatchling yellow-rimmed box turtles, Cuora flavomarginata, are very pretty and very alert.

collected and imported from China. Determined by availability, the price of this species fluctuates wildly.

Habits: This is a colorful and, once acclimated, outgoing and hardy species of box turtle. However, new imports are very shy and may remain tightly closed within their shells for hours. We have found all to be most active during rainstorms and barometric pressure drops that accompany passing frontal systems.

Appearance: The shell of this basically terrestrial species is moderately to highly domed and the concentric growth rings remain prominent, unless physically worn from the shell by abrasion. The carapacial color of the yellow-rimmed box turtle is somewhat variable—brown, olive-brown, or black.

There is usually a rather prominent vertebral stripe and the marginals are yellow on their undersides; from the yellow rim both common and specific names are derived. The head is very prettily colored. The olive-gray to olive-brown of the crown is separated from the yellow-green of the cheeks by a yellow (sometimes greenish yellow) stripe that is thinly delineated by a darker edging. The lower cheeks and chin shade to a pale peach to brighter yellow. The legs are dark, the axillae yellowish. This is another turtle species that is very difficult to sex. The tail of both sexes is short, but that of the male is comparatively wider at the base. The posterior lobe of the male's plastron is straight in side view and rounded when viewed from above. The corresponding plastral lobe of the female is slightly-more angular and the posterior tip may curve slightly upward when viewed from the side. Most of our adults are between 4.5 and 5.5 inches (11–14 cm) in carapace length.

This is an omnivorous turtle species. Ripe and overripe fruits, worms, cat foods, mice, and nearly any other edible thing are eagerly consumed.

Breeding: Our female yellow-margined box turtles have several nestings annually of either a single egg or a pair of eggs. The nests are very shallow and the layings are separated by from 10 to 18 days. In Florida we have always allowed nature to take its course and find hatchlings in the yard from late summer to very late fall; we make no effort to provide heat or additional lighting for the turtles. Here the cycling and nesting are all accomplished naturally.

Diet and Housing

Box turtles are popularly thought to be among the most ideal of pet turtles. And they are—after they have been acclimated to captive conditions. One of the things that makes box turtles so desirable to so many people is the fact that they eat a wide range of food. This, too, is true. Box turtles are not entirely frugivorous, nor are fruits even the favorite food of many specimens. This can easily be seen by the initial attitude of many new captives toward fruit. They'll walk all around it, some may even sniff it—but they won't eat it!

But if you want to induce a recalcitrant newly acquired eastern box turtle to feed, try a night crawler. The box turtle will almost jump on the worm in its haste to feed! Western box turtles are less enthusiastic about worms, but are usually instantaneously interested in—are you ready for this?—dung beetles, as well as crickets and locusts. Once the turtle is feeding well, it can be weaned over to canned cat foods and fresh fruit, berries, and mushrooms. Treats of worms and crickets will always be appreciated though.

Winter: Although box turtles can be kept indoors, they are more suited to an outdoor existence. No matter at what latitude you live, if you can provide the correct humidity (high for eastern and Asian box turtles, low for westerns), box turtles will thrive out of doors during summer weather. However, how you prepare the turtles for winter will vary by species and latitude.

Asian, Gulf Coast, Florida, and southernmost individuals of other species and subspecies will require no period of hibernation; thus, at northern latitudes, these are best housed indoors for the winter. However, if you live in the lower Rio Grande valley or peninsular Florida, modifications can be made that will enable you to keep the turtles outside year-round. They may be inactive for a few days during the passing of strong cold fronts. Again, we refer you to our comments on hibernation, beginning on page 25.

Male tortoises (like this red-foot) and some turtles have a plastral concavity that helps them maintain balance when breeding.

The True Tortoises

With but a single exception, the true tortoises (family Testudinidae) are moderately to highly domed terrestrial turtles ranging from small— 2.5 inches (6 cm), to huge—more than 40 inches (100 cm). The single exception to the domed carapace is the curiously flattened pancake tortoise, *Malacochersus tornieri*, of eastern Africa. Most tortoises live more than 25 years, and many far longer than that, a factor to consider when you think about obtaining one.

Until the mid-1980s, tortoises were rather readily available and quite inexpensive. Today this is no longer the case. Most tortoises are now protected by international law or regulation. Many species once commonly seen are no longer available, a few are sporadically so, and if exportation for the pet trade is allowed, it is usually on a quota system. The result of the curtailed

This red-footed tortoise, Chelonoidis carbonaria, *is of typical appearance and has been in captivity for more than 35 years.*

importation has been higher prices and greater interest in captive-breeding projects.

Size: It is important to consider several things when you purchase a tortoise. Among these is the space available (if you have only a 2–4 foot (.6–1.2 m) cage you should not purchase a spur-thighed tortoise, *Geochelone sulcata*, which may near 100 pounds (45 kg) in weight when it is adult).

If you live in the humid Southeast you might wish to rethink your pending purchase of an

Hatchling yellow-footed tortoises have strongly serrate marginal scutes.

arid-land tortoise, such as the Egyptian tortoise, *Testudo kleinmanni.*

Unless you have enough space for large tortoises, tailor your choice of specimens to conditions available. If you live in a humid area (or a fog belt) consider the red-footed or yellow-footed tortoise, *Chelonoidis carbonaria* or *Chelonoidis denticulata.* For small indoor facilities buy small tortoise species. *Testudo hermanni,* the Herrmann's tortoise, is one of the better species; the elongated tortoise, *Indotestudo elongata*, is another. If you do have a fair expanse of yard that you can dedicate to a tortoise area and if you live in Florida, Texas's Rio Grande valley, or other perpetually hot area, and if you enjoy larger tortoises, you have a lot of choices. A Leopard tortoise, *G. pardalis*, a spur-thighed tortoise, or even an Aldabra tortoise, *Aldabrachelys gigantea*, may be just the ticket. All are now captive-bred in fair numbers.

Diet: Tortoises are largely, but not exclusively, herbivorous. In the wild, many will consume carrion, insects, or even nestling rodents or birds if they happen across them. Captives of most species will eagerly eat dark leafy vegetables (romaine, escarole), pulpy fruit (such as squashes), fruits (apples, pears, kiwis, tomatoes) and a very little prepared tortoise diet or dog kibble. There are several tortoise diets now on the market that claim to offer complete nutrition, but we would still recommend variety. We know that the fruit/veggie diet works, for we've had some of our tortoises for more than 40 years. We periodically add a D_3-calcium supplement to the food. Vitamin/mineral supplements are given to rapidly growing young tortoises more frequently than to adults.

Breeding: Many tortoises will breed year-round; others (especially species from temperate areas or tropical areas having well-defined rainy and dry seasons) have one or two circumscribed breeding seasons annually. In most cases breeding will occur in the spring when the hours of daylight are increasing, or at the advent of

the rainy seasons. Low barometric pressure (if accompanied by suitably warm temperatures) may stimulate breeding year-round.

Nesting is a lengthy process for the stub-toed tortoises. Depending on soil composition, it may take a species such as a radiated tortoise, *Geochelone radiata*, from two to four hours to complete the nesting sequence.

If the soil in one spot is unsatisfactory for nesting, the tortoise usually moves over a few feet and tries again. If the new spot doesn't work, the female is in a bit of a predicament, to put it mildly. She may retain her eggs and become egg-bound. Veterinary intervention is needed in such cases.

Gopher tortoises, *Gopherus polyphemus*, may take a shorter time for nest preparation, but they often dig their nests in the yielding sand aprons that front their burrows.

Egg incubation may be divided into two types: low humidity and high humidity (please see comments on incubation, pages 30–31).

South American Tortoises

Despite its vast continental expanse, South America has comparatively few tortoises. The two that we continue to see with some degree of regularity are the red-footed and the yellow-footed tortoises. These two species do well in humid situations. The red-foot is both a savanna and forest-edge species, while the yellow-foot seems more restricted to forests.

Range: The natural range of the red-footed tortoise is from Panama to Argentina (mostly east of the Andes) and some West Indian Islands. Within that range there is much variation in adult size and color. Breeders and dealers often designate color or shell form when offering their red-footed tortoises. You may see reference to red-headed or cherry-headed" red-foots, to "Bolivian giants," or to "Colombians" (these latter have prominently concave shell sides), or any of several other designations. The prices of some are higher than those of others, but none is inexpensive any longer.

Appearance: Although many are smaller, red-foots often attain a foot (30 cm) in length and some near 18 inches (45 cm). The elongate shell is highly domed, of a dark ground color and, when viewed from above, has parallel to concave sides. The anterior marginals, even of hatchlings, are nonserrate. There is a light yellow to orange spot in the center of each of the costal and vertebral scutes, and a less well-defined light spot often occurs on each marginal. The scales of the head and forelimbs may vary from yellow through orange to red. Typically, the scales of the forelimbs are brighter than those of the head.

Yellow-footed tortoises attain a much greater size than the rather closely allied red-foot. In bygone days some of the yellow-footed tortoises seen in the pet trade were close to 30 inches (76 cm) in shell length. Apparently they came from the forested tri-country area of Amazonian Colombia, Peru, and Brazil.

Today, only seldom are wild-collected yellow-foots of great size available. Almost all specimens offered for sale are captive-bred hatchlings. Babies are round when viewed from above but elongate with maturity. The carapace color is yellowish, often with gray or brown overtones. The scales of the head and forelimbs are yellow. Anterior marginals are serrate.

Both the red-footed and yellow-footed tortoises are very hardy and pretty species that we strongly recommend as starter tortoises. Of course, there are many very advanced hobbyists who prize these species, too. We do urge that you acquire captive-hatched babies whenever possible.

Breeding: Even the hatchlings are hardy and readily accept a variety of food. As the tortoises approach sexual maturity, you will note that males are often less highly domed and have a broader carapace than the females. Males also have a concave plastron and a heavier, longer tail than females.

Courtship involves a species-specific series of head bobs and nods as well a series of chuckling vocalizations. After immobilizing the female by nipping her shell and limbs, the male mounts and breeds her. Small to moderate clutches (3 to 10 eggs) are usually produced by adult females. In the "humid" incubator at 82–86°F (28–30°C), incubation varies from 100 to nearly 180 days.

African Tortoises

The African continent is home to many diverse tortoise species. Some are small; some are large. Some have an immense range and others not only have a small range, but are locally distributed as well. Only a few African species are readily available in the pet trade, and of these some are difficult to maintain as captives. We will discuss the arid-land dwelling North African spur-thighed tortoise, *Testudo graeca* ssp. and the African spurred tortoise, *Geochelone sulcata*, as well as the savanna-dwelling leopard tortoise, *Geochelone pardalis* ssp. We will also make mention of the diverse and difficult-to-maintain hinge-backed tortoises (*Kinxys* sp.) and the very specialized little pancake tortoise, *Malacochersus tornieri*. It is important that the reader not confuse the North African spur-thighed tortoises with the sub-Saharan African spurred tortoise.

The similarity of the common names is a perfect example of why it is better to learn and use scientific names of reptiles and amphibians.

The Spur-thighed tortoise is not as commonly seen in the pet trade today as in past years. However, it is still one of the more commonly encountered forms. Pet trade trafficking is probably directly responsible for severely depleting populations of this turtle in many areas of its range. Fortunately, despite wild-collected adults still being the most commonly seen and inexpensive, a number of hobbyists are now breeding the several difficult-to-identify subspecies of this little tortoise. Although some examples may near a foot (30 cm) in size, most are between 6 and 8 inches (15-20 cm) long when adult.

T. graeca can be difficult to acclimate to captive conditions, especially in cool but perpetually humid areas. When maintenance is attempted in such areas, respiratory ailments are not uncommon. Despite treatment, these often worsen or reoccur and can be fatal. It is somewhat easier to succeed with this tortoise species in dry-to-arid regions.

To do best with this species, it is necessary to know where your specimen originated. In some areas of its range this tortoise hibernates (brumates) in winter and estivates in excessively hot summer weather. In other areas it may do one or the other, and specimens in yet other populations remain active year-round.

The most successful breeders of the various *Testudo* species advocate an entirely herbivorous diet.

Range: *T. graeca* may be found from seashore dunes to rocky mountain steppes at considerable elevations. It is most often associated with sparsely vegetated, dry areas but may occasionally wander temporarily into damper areas. Typi-

Brilliant yellow markings on a black carapace are a recurring theme on many Asiatic and African tortoises. This is a hatchling star tortoise, Geochelone elegans.

cally, these tortoises are most active in the morning.

Appearance: While they are certainly not brightly colored, spur-thighed tortoises are variable and attractive. The ground color is tan to horn and patches of dark pigment usually are present. In some populations the dark coloration predominates. The head is dark, the limbs light, and a projecting conical tubercle, the "spur" from which the common name is derived, is present on each side of the tail.

Breeding: The techniques needed to cycle this tortoise for breeding will vary. In some cases, considerable winter cooling may be necessary but, in the case of tortoises from nonhibernating populations, hibernating the tortoise may do far more harm than good. Breeding, an affair where the male butts, shoves, and bites the female, occurs in the spring of the year. Nesting occurs several weeks later. From one to a dozen eggs are laid. Some females dig well-formed, substantial nests; others (at least in captivity) may do little more than dig a shallow depression and place a dusting of earth over the eggs laid therein. Some females may produce more than a single clutch in a season.

African Spurred Tortoise

In contrast to the spur-thighed tortoise, the African spurred tortoise is an immense beast. Some males near 30 inches (90 cm) in length and may exceed 120 pounds (50 kg) in weight. Unfortunately, despite its not being a suitable tortoise for most pet keepers, this animated bull-dozer is bred in large numbers and is available at very modest prices.

The shell of this tortoise is usually an unmarked tan to brown (ivory colored examples are now also being bred) with darker growth areas between the carapacial scutes. It is a hardy, adaptable, and usually personable species. The sexes are rather difficult to differentiate, but females are smaller than males, have the smaller tail, and do not have the weak plastral concavity of most males.

Hatchlings have somewhat brighter hues than adults, but this is a comparison only. When properly cared for, hatchlings grow very rapidly. They reach large sizes and sexual maturity in just a few years. When you are considering the purchase of babies, their adult size and the caging space required by adults should be kept in mind. As mentioned earlier, the range of this, the largest of the world's mainland tortoises, runs roughly along the southern edge of the Sahara Desert. Thus, in nature it is an arid-land species.

There are two forms of leopard tortoise, the very large Geochelone p. pardalis *(left) and the smaller and more northerly* G. p. babcocki. *Hatchlings of the former usually have two dark spots in each carapacial scute.*

Additionally, it is an accomplished burrower. Some examples will dig a burrow 4 feet (1.2 m) deep and more than 20 feet (6 m) long. Other specimens, though, may merely push their way beneath a shrub and make a shallow pallet to which they regularly retire.

Breeding: African spurred tortoises breed readily in captivity. Females dig well-formed, deep nesting holes. The clutch size varies from 5 to about 18 eggs, but 7 to 10 seems most common. Several clutches are laid annually. Females often dig well down into the soil with their rear before reversing position and digging the actual nesting chamber with their rear feet. At temperatures of 83 to 86°F (28–30°C) incubation lasts for about three months. In nature, incubation durations of up to seven months have been reported.

Note: The purchase of this tortoise should be considered only if you live in a region where it can be kept outside year-round.

Leopard tortoises, Geochelone pardalis ssp., are available in two questionably valid subspecies. These are often designated the Babcock's leopard tortoise, *G. p. babcocki,* and the giant leopard tortoise, *G. p. pardalis.* It is the smaller Babcock's form that is most commonly available in the pet trade. This race occurs over much of southern Africa (except for the southwestern section). Although some specimens may attain slightly more than a 2-foot (61 cm) shell length, most are much smaller.

Breeding: Females of 1 foot (30 cm) in length are known to produce viable eggs that have been fertilized by males even smaller.

Males of the giant leopard tortoise often attain a length of 20 inches (66 cm) and a weight of 50 pounds (21 kg) is not uncommon. This large form occurs in southwestern South Africa.

Female leopard tortoises dig deep, well-formed nests. Multiple clutches are usually produced by each sexually active female. Each clutch is separated from the last by three- to four-week intervals. Each clutch may contain from 4 to 14 (by small females) to more than 30 (by larger females) eggs. While the eggs of Babcock's leopard tortoise have proven easy to successfully incubate in a low-humidity incubator set at 86°F (30°C), those of the giant form have proven more problematic. Babcock's leopard tortoise eggs hatch in about 3 months. Most success has been had with giant leopard tortoise eggs when they are left in the ground to incubate naturally. The incubation duration of naturally incubated giant leopard tortoise eggs is from 9 months to nearly a year.

Hatchlings leopard tortoises are beautifully and contrastingly colored in light yellow and black. Sexual differences are rather slight. The adult male does have a weak plastral concavity (not present in females) and the tail is somewhat longer and heavier than that of the female.

Habitat: The natural habitat of the leopard tortoise is variable (open woodlands, scrub, grasslands, and savannas) but always in rather arid, well-drained areas. Some specimens adapt rather readily to humid conditions (the southeastern United States or isolated fog belts elsewhere) but many will require lengthy acclimatization. Where conditions are cold and damp, this species seems rather susceptible to respiratory problems. However, once acclimatized, and if otherwise properly cared for, these tortoises will live for several decades in captivity. Because of their large adult size, leopard tortoises are best maintained outside whenever possible.

Appearance: In coloration leopard tortoises may vary from sparsely to heavily patterned. The namesake leopard spots are present only on juvenile specimens. These fragment with advanc-

ing age and other more irregular markings may form. The edges of each scute are usually the lightest in color. The ground color is tan, yellow, or (when adult) some shade of dusty brown. The smudges are black.

Moderate carapacial pyramiding is not uncommon, and may be seen in some wild specimens. The carapaces of both the leopard tortoise and the African spurred tortoise species normally retain prominent growth rings.

Diet: Leopard and spur-thighed tortoises are preferentially vegetarians and have prodigious appetites. Wild specimens eat many types of grasses, succulents, and fungi. Captives eat many kinds of available greens, pulpy vegetables, and fruits. A very little high-quality prepared tortoise chow can also be offered. Excesses of animal protein in the diet have now been linked to reptilian gout.

The little East African pancake (or soft-shelled tortoise), *Malacochersus tornieri*, is the most remarkable of the world's tortoises. It is a flattened species tortoise that is adult at only 4.5 to 6 inches (11.4–15.2 cm) in length.

Appearance: The carapace is of some shade of tan or brown, and radiating markings of variable intensity may or may not be present.

Breeding: A single egg is produced at each nesting, but several nestings occur annually. With such a low reproductive rate, the onslaught of collecting for the pet trade has severely depleted some populations. It is now been bred in captivity. Incubation takes several months in a low-humidity incubator at 84 to 86°F (28.8–30°C). Hatchlings are proportionately much more highly domed than the adults.

If provided with dry warm quarters this little vegetarian is a hardy and easily kept species. It will eat grasses and both leafy and pulpy vegeta-

The little pancake tortoise, **Malacochersus tornieri** *is a divergent, flat-shelled tortoise.*

bles in captivity. Augmentation of this diet with some fruit is acceptable. In natural habitat, the pancake tortoise is an agile denizen of arid, rock-strewn savannas. (Yes! A tortoise can be agile!) The pliable shell allows the tortoise to avoid predators by entering narrow fissures where it then holds itself in place with its strongly clawed limbs. It is now known that the pancake tortoise does not wedge itself in place by inflating its lungs and expanding its height, as once thought.

Hinge-Backed Tortoises

All hinge-backed tortoises belong to the genus *Kinixys.* Some species (the Bell's and Speik's hinge-backs) are denizens of dry savannah habitats. Others (Home's and forest hinge-backs) inhabit much damper tropical African habitats. Whether from dry or damp regions, because they are often in deplorable condition when they are imported, hinge-backed tortoises can be difficult to acclimate to captive conditions. If you choose

to acquire a hinge-back, ascertain that it has good weight, clear eyes, and have a veterinarian check it for internal parasites before completing the purchase.

Appearance: Hinge-backs are interesting tortoises that are elongate and most are highly domed. The anterior marginal scutes flare upward and the rear marginals may flare outward. The carapace bears a functional hinge between the 4th and the 5th costal scutes. This allows the rear of the carapace to be lowered against the end of the plastron, thus protecting the tail and hind limbs.

Food: Although omnivorous, hinge-backs are very fond of worms and insects. They will also eat a variety of fruits and vegetables.

Habitat: The habitat provided by you will necessarily vary according to the species of hinge-back that you acquire. Those from dry savannas will require warmth, low humidity, and drinking water, while those from forest habitats must be provided with warmth and high humidity, and a shallow soaking tray (that must always be kept clean) from which the tortoises will also drink.

These tortoises are bred by very few hobbyists. Those available in the pet trade are wild-collected imported specimens. A clutch contains 2 to 4 eggs. It is not known whether only a single cluch or multiple clutches are produced annually. Eggs are laid on the ground surface amid vegetational debris.

Asian Tortoises

Although there are many species of tortoises indigenous to Asia, few are now available in the pet trade. We will discuss only two species, the star tortoise, *Geochelone elegans,* and the elongated tortoise, *G. elongata.*

Home's hinge-backed tortoise, **Kinixys** **homeana,** *is one of two forest-dwelling hinge-backed species.*

The Star Tortoise

The star tortoise, *Geochelone elegans*, is adult at a length of from 6 to 11 inches (15–28 cm). It is now captive-bred in fair numbers. This is one of the most beautiful of the world's tortoise species. Its black shell is elongate, highly domed, and vividly marked on each scute with a series of bright yellow radiations. It is indigenous to India, Sri Lanka, and Pakistan and is associated with relatively humid forested areas. It either forages early in the day or is quiescent during dry periods, but it may wander, feed, and breed throughout the daylight hours during the rains and monsoons. The largest specimens are found in Sri Lanka.

Breeding: Males of this beautiful tortoise are very aggressive, both toward other males and toward females during breeding attempts. Considerable ramming, butting, and biting is indulged in. Wheezing chuckles are voiced by breeding males.

Star tortoises dig deep, flasked nests in which from 2 to 10 (usually 4 to 6) eggs are placed. In a humid incubator, at 84 to 86°F (28.8–30°C), incubation lasts from 85 to 95 days. Natural incubation may be nearly two months longer. The babies are vividly colored but not as intricately patterned as the adults.

The Elongated Tortoise

In direct contrast to the star tortoise, the elongated tortoise, *Indotestudo elongata*, is also adult at about a foot (30 cm) in length. It has a ground color of horn and may or may not be smudged with black. It is not a colorful species, but it is alert, hardy, and rather regularly available. It is interesting that the skin of the nose

breeding. They must be kept separated at all other times. The nest of this species is small, at times being barely large enough to fully accommodate the 2 to 4 eggs. At 86°F (30°C) elongated tortoise eggs hatch after about 100 days of incubation.

This is another forest species that is fond of high humidity. It is found from India and surrounding countries to Vietnam and Malaysia.

and around the eyes becomes suffused with rose-red during the breeding season. This seems brightest on male specimens. The carapace is highly domed, but is somewhat flattened dorsally. Elongated tortoises are now captive bred in small numbers.

Breeding: This species, too, is an aggressive breeder. Some males are so persistently aggressive toward females that they can be only temporarily housed together for the purpose of

American Tortoises

There are three species of true tortoises indigenous to the United States. All are in the genus Gopherus. All are protected either by state law (Texas tortoise, *G. berlandieri*) or both state and federal laws (gopher, *G. polyphemus*, and desert, *G. agassizii*, tortoises). Permits are necessary before any of these can be legally collected or kept. In comparison with other tortoise species, our three native ones can be difficult to acclimate (especially if removed from natural habitat conditions) and all should be considered basically outdoor species. The gopher tortoise excavates extensive burrows. Some populations of the desert tortoise also make long burrows but others simply take shelter beneath vegetation. The Texas tortoise usually just plows shallow pallets into the earth beneath or against a shrub or clump of cacti.

Diet: All three species are primarily vegetarian. Much of their food in the wild consists of harsh

The elongated tortoise may or may not have dark smudges on its olive-tan shell.

grasses and other similar vegetation. Morning glories, succulents, fruit and blossoms also figure prominently in the diet of all. The adult size ranges from 6 inches (15 cm) (Texas tortoise) to more than 12 inches (30 cm) (gopher and desert tortoises). All are brown to black when adult but more colorful as hatchlings. Growth annuli are usually retained by all three species throughout their long lives.

Of the three, the desert tortoises are most frequently seen. They have lived for more than five decades in captivity. Contact the Game and Fish Commissions in your individual states for permit information.

European Tortoises

Hermann's Tortoise

Testudo hermanni ssp.

This is a long-time hobbyist favorite. The western race, *T. h. hermanni* is adult at 6 to 7 inches (15–17.5 cm) in length, of dull coloration. It often lacks strongly contrasting markings. The eastern race, *T. h. boettgeri*, is more brightly colored and larger—up to 11 inches (35.5 cm).

Range: Hermann's tortoise ranges widely in suitably dry habitats on both the southern European mainland and on many of the adjacent islands. It favors open woodlands and scrub and dry areas overgrown by grasses and herbaceous plants.

Appearance: The carapace of *T. hermanni* is highly domed and hued in a ground color of horn. Black markings, variable in size, shape, and quantity are usually present. The posterior lobe of the plastron is weakly hinged.

Diet: Hermann's tortoise is primarily a vegetarian, eating the typical tortoise fare of dark

Western Hermann's tortoises, testudo h. hermanni, are small and quite cold tolerant.

leafy vegetables, pulpy vegetables (such as squash), broccoli stems and leaves, flowers, and some fruit. This tortoise particularly favors clovers, dandelions and buttercups. Some specimens will prey on insects and other invertebrates as well as their more usual herbs and grasses.

Breeding: Hermann's tortoise has been bred by both European and American hobbyists for many decades. Brumation is probably necessary for the long-term physiological well-being and breeding of this species. Males breed the females aggressively, butting and biting to immobilize their mates. Nests are flasked and about 4 inches (10 cm) deep. Several clutches of from 2 to 10 (occasionally more) eggs are laid annually by adult females. At from 83 to 86°F (28.3–30°C) incubation takes from 80 to 100 days. The hatchlings are hardy and grow quickly. It is suggested that minimal animal matter be fed the hatchlings of this tortoise species.

GLOSSARY

Albino Lacking black pigment.

Alveolar ridge (or plate) A broad crushing plate posterior to the mandibles.

Ambient temperature The temperature of the surrounding environment.

Anterior Toward the front.

Anus The external opening of the cloaca; the vent.

Bridge The "bridge of shell" between forelimbs and rear limbs that connects the carapace and the plastron.

Brumation The reptilian and amphibian equivalent of mammalian hibernation.

Carapace The upper shell of a chelonian.

Caudal Pertaining to the tail.

cb/cb Captive-bred, captive-born.

cb/ch Captive-bred, captive-hatched.

Chelonian A turtle or tortoise.

Chorioallantois The gas-permeable membranous layer inside the shell of a reptile egg.

Circadian rhythm Twenty-four hour cycle of biological activity.

Cloaca The common chamber into which digestive, urinary, and reproductive systems empty and which itself opens exteriorly through the vent or anus.

Congener A member of the same genus.

Crepuscular Active at dusk and/or dawn.

Debridement Surgical removal of diseased tissue.

Deposition As used here, the laying of the eggs or birthing of young.

Deposition site The nesting site.

Dimorphic A difference in form, build, or coloration involving the same species; often sex-linked.

Diurnal Active in the daytime.

Dorsal Pertaining to the back; upper surface.

Dorsum The upper surface.

Ecological niche The precise habitat utilized by a species.

Ectothermic Cold-blooded; lacking internal body temperature regulation.

Endemic Confined to a specific region.

Endothermic Warm-blooded.

Erythristic Having a prevailing red pigment.

Estivation A period of warm weather inactivity, often triggered by excessive heat or drought.

Form An identifiable species or subspecies.

Genus A taxonomic classification of a group of species having similar characteristics. The genus falls between the next broader designation of "family" and the next narrower designation of "species." Genera is the plural of genus. The genus is always capitalized.

Glottis The opening of the windpipe.

Gravid The reptilian equivalent of mammalian pregnancy.

Gular Pertaining to the throat.

Heliothermic Pertaining to a species that basks in the sun to thermoregulate.

Herpetoculture The captive breeding of reptiles and amphibians.

Herpetoculturist One who engages in herpetoculture.

Herpetologist One who engages in herpetology.

Herpetology The study (often scientifically oriented) of reptiles and amphibians.

Hibernaculum (pl. hibernacula) A winter den.

Hibernation Winter dormancy.

Hybrid Offspring resulting from the breeding of two species.

Hydrate To restore body moisture by drinking or absorption.

Immaculate Without colored spots.

Intergrade Offspring resulting from the breeding of two subspecies.

Juvenile A young or immature specimen.

Keel A carapacial or plastral ridge.
Lateral Pertaining to the side.
Mandibles Jaws.
Mandibular Pertaining to the jaws.
Melanism A profusion of black pigment.
Middorsal Pertaining to the middle of the back.
Monotypic Containing but one type.
Nocturnal Active at night.
Ocellus (pl. ocelli) An eyespot or eyelike colored spot.
Ontogenetic Maturation-related (color) changes.
Oviparous Reproducing by means of eggs that hatch after laying.
Pathogen A specific disease-causing agent.
Photoperiod The daily/seasonally variable length of the hours of daylight.
Plastron The bottom shell.
Poikilothermic (also ectothermic) A species with no internal body temperature regulation. The old term was "cold-blooded."
Postocular To the rear of the eye.
Race A subspecies.
Saxicolous Rock-dwelling.
Scute Scale.
Species A group of similar creatures that produce viable young when breeding. The taxonomic designation narrower than genus and broader than subspecies. Abbreviation, sp.
Stomatitis Mouth infection.
Subspecies The subdivision of a species. A race that may differ slightly in color, size, scalation, or other criteria. Abbreviation, ssp.
Substrate The physical base on which an animal or plant lives.
Sympatric Occurring in the same range without interbreeding.
Taxon (pl. taxa) A classified group of animals or plants.

Eastern chicken turtles are narrow-shelled and long necked. They feed on fish, invertebrates, and crustaceans.

Taxonomy The science of classification of plants and animals.
Terrestrial Land-dwelling.
Thermoregulate To regulate (body) temperature by choosing a warmer or cooler environment.
Tricarinate Having a triple keel.
Vent The external opening of the cloaca; the anus.
Venter The underside of a creature; the belly.
Ventral Pertaining to the undersurface or belly.
Xeric Characterized by dryness.

INFORMATION

Turtle and Tortoise Clubs

There are several turtle and tortoise clubs in major cities in North America and Europe. Additionally, there are trusts dedicated to the conservation and preservation of the world's chelonians. Among the members and trustees are amateur enthusiasts and professional cheloniophiles. Most of the organizations produce informative newsletters and actively try to promote chelonian conservation and "chelonioculture." All welcome inquiries and new members.

California Turtle and Tortoise Club
Check Web site *www.tortoise.org/cttc/member.html* for pertinent addresses

San Diego Turtle and Tortoise Society
P.O. Box 712514
Santee, CA 92072

The New York Turtle and Tortoise Society
Membership
P.O. Box 878
Orange, NJ 07051

National Tortoise and Turtle Society
P.O. Box 66935
Phoenix, AZ 85082

Desert Tortoise Preserve Committee
4067 Mission Inn Avenue
Riverside, CA 92501

Society for the Study of Amphibians
    and Reptiles
c/o Breck Bartholomew
SSAR Publications Secretary
P.O. Box 58517
Salt Lake City, UT 84158

Gopher Tortoise Council
c/o Florida Museum of Natural History
P.O. Box 117800
Gainesville, FL 32611

Herpetologist's League Inc.
Division of Biological Sciences
Emporia State University
Emporia, Kansas 66801

Fellow amateurs and professionals may also be found at the biology departments of museums, universities, high schools, and nature centers.

The Turtles and Tortoises classified sections of *www.kingsnake.com* are immensely helpful in finding and comparing prices on both common and rare chelonian species. That website also has interactive forums on which you can ask and receive answers to questions.

Occasionally turtles (like this red-eared slider) are born with two heads.

The Cumberland terrapin, Trachemys scripta troosti, *often lack enlarged red or yellow patches on the face.*

Books

Bartlett, Richard D. *In Search of Reptiles and Amphibians.* Leiden: E. J. Brill, 1988.

———. *Digest for the Successful Terrarium.* Morris Plains, NJ: TetraPress, 1989.

Conant, Roger & Joseph T. Collins. *Reptiles and Amphibians, Eastern/Central North America.* Boston: Houghton Mifflin, 1991.

Ernst, Carl H. et al. *Turtles of the United States and Canada.* Washington, DC: Smithsonian Inst. Press, 1994.

———. & R. W. Barbour. *Turtles of the World.* Washington, DC: Smithsonian Inst. Press, 1989.

Highfield, A. C. *Tortoise Trust Guide to Tortoises and Turtles,* 2nd ed., London: Carapace Press, 1994.

Stebbins, Robert C. *A Field Guide to Western Reptiles and Amphibians.* Boston: Houghton Mifflin, 1985.

Wilke, Hartmut. Turtles, *A Complete Pet Owner's Guide.* Hauppauge, NY: Barron's Educational Series, Inc., 1983.

Hobbyist Magazines

Reptiles
P.O. Box 6050
Mission Viejo, CA 92690

Although not brightly colored, the West African mud turtle, Pelusios castaneus, *fits our definition of cuteness quite well.*

INDEX

Page numbers set in boldface type indicate photographs.

About the Authors

R. D. Bartlett is a herpetologist who has authored more than 650 articles and 10 books, and coauthored an additional 30 books. He lectures extensively and has participated in field studies across North and Latin America. In 1978 he began the Reptilian Breeding and Research Institute, a private facility. Since its inception, more than 150 species of reptiles and amphibians have been bred at RBRI, some for the first time in the United States under captive conditions. Successes at the RBRI include several endangered species.

R. D. Bartlett is a member of numerous herpetological and conservation organizations, a cohost on an on-line reptile and amphibian forum, and a contributing editor of *Reptiles* magazine.

Patricia Bartlett is a biologist and historian who has authored six books and coauthored 40 books. A museum administrator for the last fifteen years, she has worked in both history and science museums. She received the America Public Works Association Heritage Award in 1985 and serves in numerous local and state organizations.

Acknowledgments

To Bill Love, Rob MacInnes, Randy Babb, Randy Limburg, and Chris McQuade we owe a debt of gratitude for allowing us to photograph many common and uncommon turtles and tortoises. Jim Harding has provided us with slides and much information regarding the worsening plight of the American pond turtles in their natural habitats. We wish also to express appreciation to Kenny Wray, Barry Mansell, Tom Tyning and Carl May for companionship in the field.

Important Note

While handling turtles and tortoises you may occasionally receive bites or scratches. If your skin is broken, see your physician immediately.

Turtles and tortoises may transmit certain infections to humans. Always wash your hands carefully after handling your specimens and always supervise children who wish to observe your turtles and/or tortoises.

Photo Credits

All photos © R. D. Bartlett.

All inquiries should be addressed to:
Barron's Educational Series, Inc.
250 Wireless Boulevard
Hauppauge, NY 11788
www.barronseduc.com

ISBN-13: 978-0-7641-3400-5
ISBN-10: 0-7641-3400-0

Library of Congress Catalog Card No. 2006040101

Library of Congress Cataloging-in-Publication Data
Bartlett, Richard D., 1938–
   Turtles and tortoises / R. D. Bartlett and
Patricia P. Bartlett.
      p. cm. — (A complete pet owner's manual)
   Includes bibliographical references and index.
   ISBN-13: 978-0-7641-3400-5
   ISBN-10: 0-7641-3400-0
   1. Turtles as pets. I. Bartlett, Patricia Pope,
1949– II. Title. III. Series.

SF459.T8B37   2006
639.3'92—dc22   2006040101

Printed in China
9 8 7 6 5 4 3